SAILING AMONG THE STARS

✦

The Story of *Sea Dart*

SAILING AMONG THE STARS

The Story of *Sea Dart*

Laurel Wagers

SHERIDAN HOUSE

Published 1999 by
Sheridan House Inc.
145 Palisade Street
Dobbs Ferry, New York 10522

Library of Congress Cataloging-in-Publication Data

Wagers, Laurel.
    Sailing among the stars : the story of Sea Dart / Laurel Wagers.
        p.   cm.
    ISBN 1-57409-070-4 (alk. paper)
    1. Sea Dart (Boat)   2. Voyages and travels.   I. Title.
    G530.S383W34   1999
    910.4'1—dc21   99-35851
                                                              CIP

Editor: Janine Simon
Designer: Kirby J. Kiskadden

Printed in the United States of America

ISBN 1-57409-070-4

CONTENTS

Introduction

Cold winds from the north greet a cargo ship at the Bayonne, New Jersey, docks, as she releases a procession of cars and yachts from her hold. At last a tiny boat shape appears, a battered cutter with three keels. A sailor waits for her on the dock, eyes misting as he sees the familiar form for the first time in more than eighteen months.

"You go to sea in *that*?" exclaims the longshoreman at his side. He is the first of many Americans to fall under the spell of *Sea Dart*.

Twenty-one years later, on the east side of Lake Union in the heart of Seattle, Washington, the same little cutter is being loaded on a flatbed trailer for another journey inland. The manager in the office asks where she's going. When the answer is "Idaho," he remarks that it's a long trip.

"Not for this boat," his customer replies. "She crossed South America . . ."

And in seconds the previously calm and collected businessman is sitting in the boat's cockpit, saying to himself, "This is *Sea Dart*! I'm sitting in *Sea Dart*!"

Spring is stealing up the mountains of Idaho; the white dots of mountain goats contrast with the rocky slopes above Lake Pend Oreille;

and a living legend is ready to sail the thousand-foot-deep south end of the lake.

The date is May 8, 1999, and Tristan Jones would be 75 years old today. Of the many boats he sailed and wrote about, *Cresswell* was scrap years ago; *Banjo* sank after being hit by a whale; *Barbara* went back to her owner, much the worse for wear; *Banjo II* met with pirates and a hurricane shortly after her new owners took possession; *Outward Leg* is reported to be abandoned on the hard in the Philippines; *Henry Wagner* was retired in Thailand.

Sea Dart, heroine of *The Incredible Voyage*, is coming out of storage and four different refit efforts to sail again — to catch the winds on the mountain lakes of Idaho, twenty-five years and thousands of miles from the scene of her most celebrated adventures in South America.

"It is not in my nature to be sentimental about a boat," Tristan Jones declared, before he met *Sea Dart*. But by the time they had crossed South America from Lima to Buenos Aires together, and she had become 'a living legend', he credited her with the success of the voyage. He said he had tears in his eyes when he sent her on to England. He spent almost two years working for her release from British customs authorities.

"Please look after *Sea Dart*," he wrote to her next owners. "She is a symbol of strength, loyalty and determination. She is one of the most unique sailing vessels in the world. I have not bestowed this vessel upon you so easily and quickly because it was easy and quick, but because she does not belong in a museum, and she could not be sold to someone as a plaything or a status symbol. It was because she has to go to hearts that go out to her."

What is this *Sea Dart* — this symbol, this legend?

She was designed for offshore cruising, but primarily in the English Channel. She might not have been meant to brave the open Atlantic, but she sailed it. She was not intended for whitewater, but she bounced through river rapids in the depths of Paraguay. And she would have sailed on to Brazil, and whatever ports Jones had in mind, had it not been for a sudden wind on the coast of Uruguay.

This is *Sea Dart*, twenty-one feet from bow to stern, seventeen feet on the waterline, seven feet wide in the beam, just over five feet from her rub rail to the bottom of her keels. She had no electronic equipment, no radio, no engine. Built as a sloop, she was modified into a cutter. Designed originally for family sailing weekends, she was modified for heavy use, sailed across an ocean, shipped, and hauled and sailed across one continent and trailered across another. She has spent far more of her 39 years moored or stored than sailing. She has borne the marks of time, weather and water, as well as the signatures of the famous.

Tristan Jones did not sail *Sea Dart* for 200,000 miles, as some have claimed. From the West Indies to Montevideo, the hard way, was roughly 8,000 miles of sailing, hauling and shipping. She didn't sail around the world; he did that with other boats.

And she didn't set both parts of his altitude sailing record. Tristan Jones himself sailed both the Dead Sea and Lake Titicaca, but not with a single boat. Jones reached the Dead Sea with *Barbara*, but Israeli officials wouldn't let him launch her there, and he had to settle for sailing on a local craft.

Other stories about *Sea Dart* and her whereabouts, like those about Tristan Jones himself, may be exaggerations or the tricks of memory. But the boat survives, the stories swirling around her like wisps of fog.

Men have, over the centuries, set out to sea in boats even smaller and less prepossessing than *Sea Dart*. St. Brendan's sixth-century coracle, or currach, would have been open and under 20 feet in diameter. Many arctic kayaks and Eskimo and Inuit umiaks are no longer than *Sea Dart*. Sailors have competed in this century to cross the Atlantic or navigate around the world ever more quickly, in ever-smaller boats.

In an era of Global Positioning System, satellites and onboard computers, fish finders and catalogs full of electronic gear, it is easy to forget that until recent decades, sailors voyaged using their own knowledge of the sea and sky, supplemented by chart and sextant. Their boats — including *Sea Dart* — were built to travel under sail, without recourse to engines; to sail with only the sun and stars as their guidance system.

In April 1998, *Sea Dart* was tethered to a corner of the dock close by the offices of Northwest Yacht Repair on Lake Union, in the marinas-

and-houseboats neighborhood that was depicted so romantically in the movie *Sleepless in Seattle*.

Among the two-story floating cottages and the fifty-foot-and-up power yachts, *Sea Dart* looked almost like a toy left out in the sun. But she was tied up carefully, a brown plastic tarp spread over her to keep off the rain, and she was bright with white paint. The carpenters said that with cleanup, interior work and a new doghouse top for the cockpit, she would be ready to sail. Sanding and varnishing would brighten her dulled trim.

They also said that she had visitors frequently; that people had been coming down to the dock — not in a stream or a crowd, but one at a time, now and then — since the word got around that she was there. People like to look at boats, and houseboats, in general; but these visitors came to see this *one* boat, to imagine themselves sitting day after day in the 46-inch-long cockpit of tiny, no-frills, low-tech 'twelve-sheets-of-plywood' *Sea Dart*.

Seeing the cockpit, with a graceful curve of tiller at hand (a replacement), allowed them to picture this little boat facing the winds and swells of the Peruvian coast, the grasping vines of the inland river, the whitewater of a rapid.

Pressed into the white-painted arch of the companion hatch was her official registry number: REG. No 307295. Yes, this was the one.

Inside, *Sea Dart* was cleared of the carefully fitted tables, the galley with its stove and sink, the lamps and the other furnishings that once had made her a home on the water. All gone, and her white-painted interior clad in dark mahogany now, from the level of the berths up the sides and across the cabin ceiling.

The interior seemed all stowage space, from the chain locker in the forepeak to the far reaches of the quarter berths and the lazarette compartment at the stern. Surely enough room for a few months' supplies: the canned goods, the bagged food such as flour and rice, plus all the spare sails and rope and assorted parts that a long sail requires, and two people and their personal gear, a shelf of books, navigational equipment, and a typewriter. The boat that had seemed spacious began to fill up in the mind's eye, and the space available for people to move around was down to the cockpit and the few feet of workspace in the galley. A tall man, or two, would fit snugly in this boat. And the whole boat, with the mast unstepped, would fit easily in many a living room.

At her stern, in a far starboard corner, was a patched spot, unpainted and dotted with little plywood blocks on the inside — the badge of South America.

Her mast was lying next to a fence onshore, her polished boom on deck. A pair of sawhorses supported the tarp, and every breeze lifted the plastic sheet so it caught almost like a sail. It seemed as if *Sea Dart* trembled with anticipation; as if she longed to dance on the lake, catch a puff of wind and skip out toward Puget Sound.

It was as if she knew that soon she would be sailing again.

High above the sea, two thousand feet up in the northern Rockies, she will sail lakes clear and blue as the Idaho sky above her. Lakes with shifting winds that recall Titicaca, and with chop like the English Channel; and long reaches from one town or school or camp to the next, with sailors to admire her and children to learn about adventure from her.

After all her adventures, she begins a new life, doing just what she was made to do.

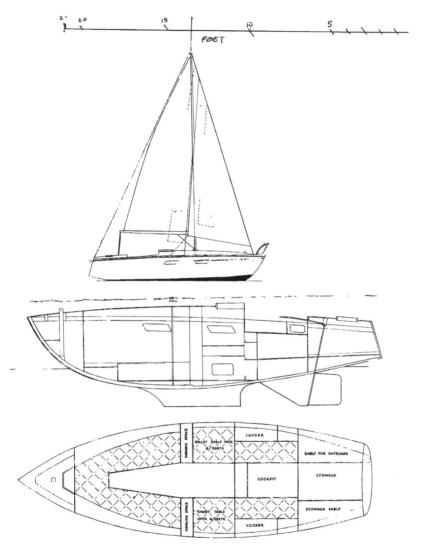

Line drawings of *Sea Dart*. COURTESY OF ROBERT TANNER.

I. Made in England

Sea Dart, built in 1960, was one of several hundred sailboats built to the Debutante design between 1959 and 1964 by Blanks Boatyard in Stanstead Abbots, Hertfordshire.

Designer Robert Tucker set out to design a boat that combined the seaworthiness required by the Junior Offshore Group, which set standards for offshore racing yachts, with the concept of a small, shallow-draft family cruiser. Tucker had made his mark with the popular Silhouette pocket cruiser in 1954, a boat which was made by the thousands. He went on to create several other modest-sized, modestly priced boats designed for British sailing conditions.

Tucker described the Debutante as "light on the helm, easy to sail, fast to windward, and comfortable to live aboard . . . a boat that has everything." Designed both for racing and cruising, the Debutante was also "docile enough to train the inexperienced in the art of seamanship." She was suited to the family budget as well, selling when new for about a thousand pounds sterling, according to a later owner. A hundred of them were sold when the Debutante design made its debut at the London Boat Show, and another hundred at the same show the next year, according to Victor Harrington, one of Blanks' boatbuilders. A small flotilla of Debutantes went to the 1962 World's Fair at Seattle.

"In the early years," the designer's son Anthony (who later took over the design firm) wrote, "the Debutante was quite an important design, as it was one of the first small plywood cruising boats that conformed to all the stability and safety requirements required of the J.O.G. (Junior Offshore Group) racing system of the time. The high volume hull by the standards in those days was innovative, providing substantial stability reserves and 'dry' boat."

Blanks Boatyard built the Debutante Mark I and Mark II. As seen on *Sea Dart*, the Mark I has a center keel and a skeg-hung rudder. For the Mark II, the ballast keel was lengthened and its weight increased by fifty pounds, and a fully balanced spade rudder replaced the earlier type. One writer noted that, since the longer, heavier keel was the only improvement between the two boats, it might behoove the owners of Mark I Debutantes to increase the ballast they carried, preferably in the form of extra beer.

Anthony Tucker also describes a Mark III version, the Gallant or Gallant 23, which was an expansion of the Debutante, with a raised doghouse that included improved ventilation. The Mark III, he said, also had a much deeper draft than the Mark I and II. Another Debutante, the Escapade, was nearly 26 feet long, with a doghouse, extended lazarette, cutter rig and deep fin keel.

After Blanks Boatyard closed in the mid-1960s, Robert Tucker modified the plans for amateur construction to produce a Debutante IV, a much simpler design than those built by professional boatbuilders. Amateurs have built more than fifty using these plans, according to Anthony Tucker.

One attribute of the Debutante class that would serve *Sea Dart* well in many of her adventures was the watertightness noted in an independent trial report by Lieutenant Commander J.F.C. Tucker, R.N. Ret. (no relation to the designer).

"[The cockpit] is surprisingly comfortable although this had been made watertight and self-draining. A feature which is most noticeable is that no water lies anywhere on the boat. The somewhat excessive camber of the decks insures that water rolls off as soon as it arrives (actually she is very dry and seldom wets her decks except for light spray) and all seats and even the cockpit floor have been ingeniously built to run off the water and drain it away."

*   *   *

Ron Reil noted dry wood shavings in *Sea Dart'*s bilge in 1971, which he took as evidence that water simply didn't enter the boat.

Tucker's report also noted the considerable stowage space, the stability of the Debutante and the pleasing shape of her hull, "a very purposeful appearance which is aerodynamically sound and immensely strong and leak-proof . . . business-like, safe and very seaworthy."

The Debutante's stability came in large part from her keels. The original Mark I specifications from the designer include a cast-iron ballast keel containing 750 pounds of lead, and two bilge keels of ⅜-inch mild-steel plate.

These bilge keels were to become common in British boat designs. Angled out like a whale's pectoral fins, the quadrilateral keels allow the boat to sit solidly on land when necessary — when the tide drops several feet and leaves the boat high and dry, for example, as on the British coast, or when she is hauled out for cleaning and painting. The three-keel design also gave the Debutante a remarkable stability in the water: Tristan Jones commented on *Sea Dart* not heeling more than thirty degrees.

Sea Dart was built somewhat differently from other Debutantes. The story is that her scantlings (specifications) were modified for an expedition through the Northwest Passage from Greenland to Alaska. This modification consisted of a generally stouter construction than other Debutantes. One visible example is that her bulkheads are made of ⅝-inch-thick plywood where ⅜-inch was specified. And she has a motor well which was not part of the original design; this could have been done at the boatyard or by one of her earlier owners. Any other modifications or obvious, dramatic variations such as metal plating on the boat were removed or lost to damage in the early 1960s.

That heavier construction may have been what saved her and her crew on the journey down the River Paraná. But by itself, it might not have been sufficient for the rigors of the Northwest Passage. Other than kayaks and umiaks, most of the boats that have taken on that passage have been heavily built. John Bockstoce, who navigated the Passage from west to east in 1983-84, chose a 60-foot-long, cutter-rigged steel motorsailer, virtually a small icebreaker.

Debutante specifications describe a boat 21 feet long overall, seven feet wide at the beam and 16 feet on the waterline, with a draft of two feet, three inches. It was designed with a sloop rig, carrying an 80-square-foot mainsail and a 75-square-foot jib, its sail area planned more for cruising in brisk winds than for speed. Its net weight was one ton. It was built mostly of marine plywood and African mahogany. Basic specifications included a cold-molded deck of ¾-inch laminated plywood, hull planking of ⅜-inch scarfed plywood, and hatches, bulkheads and interior joinery of ⅜-inch plywood framed in mahogany, with brass screws and pins, and galvanized steel bolts throughout. Stem, keel and hog were all African mahogany, as were the chines, gunwales, and toe and rub rails. The deadwood is specified as reinforced plastic.

There was no doghouse on the first Debutante models as designed. The designer commented, "Her appearance is unusual to those long accustomed to coachroofs and doghouses, but it is something of a return to an earlier age, except that modern techniques now enable us to combine uncluttered decks for safe sail-handling with above average accommodation below." Headroom in the cabin was specified as four feet, two inches, which allows an adult to sit on the cushioned berth; but even with the definite arch overhead, it's a cozy fit.

The height of the hull was another reason the Debutante stayed so dry: water didn't easily splash high enough to get into the boat.

Robert Tanner bought a Debutante Mark I in Norfolk, Virginia, from a U.S. Navy officer who had purchased the boat in England. He described her as a "rather unconventional looking boat, one of the first twin keelers on the market and ideally suited for cruising the Chesapeake Bay because of the 27-inch draft." The first owner had replaced her mast with a taller one to increase sail area and catch the lighter airs of the bay. Tanner describes *Game Pattie* as "quite a stiff boat, it handled well in rough weather, but no racehorse!" Her framing was light, with just enough 'ribs' to hold the molded plywood structure together.

James Frank Bernard Osborne bought *Sea Dart* as a bare hull, apparently in 1965, and set about refitting her to carry out a dream of adventure. Osborne, who listed his occupation on the boat's registration as trainee manager, was 24 years old at the time.

Thanks to her builders, *Sea Dart* was suited for hard use, so she was better prepared for what Osborne had in mind than some of the boats that have made the voyage.

One of his most important choices for voyaging purposes was to convert *Sea Dart* from a Bermudian sloop, as she is described in the registry, into a cutter. (Tanner also changed his Debutante's rigging, increasing the sail area to 320 square feet.) In doing so, he added a handsome bowsprit, which was supported by shrouds in the form of chains to the bow; these are clearly visible in photographs from 1971. This allowed him to add more sail area overall, and to rig a second headsail.

A sloop rig consists of mainsail and jib, with the main catching most of the wind. The cutter rig places more sail up front and balances the rigging, so the boat's sail area is divided almost equally between mainsail and headsails. Using two headsails — and having more choices of jibs, genoa, or other smaller sails — increases the boat's responsiveness to whatever wind is available, and adds flexibility so the skipper can fine-tune the sails to suit the weather. The cutter rig, with the sails operated from the cockpit, is also easier for a sailor to handle single-handed.

Another elegant touch was a pair of carved dolphins, one on either side of *Sea Dart*'s bow.

A doghouse addition gave *Sea Dart*'s crew a few inches more headroom in the galley area of the cabin; brass lamps and stove were gimballed, to stay level in any weather. Fittings were brass, shiny and golden. She was a handsome little boat.

Osborne, who lived in Romsey, Hampshire, registered *Sea Dart* with Customs and Excise in November 1965, and the registry shows that he had a mortgage on the boat with a firm in London (a mortgage, in and of itself, is one of the reasons an owner would register a boat). Four years later the mortgage was paid and the appropriate entry added to the registration.

Osborne is said to have claimed that he built *Sea Dart*. While that's not technically true, certainly he rebuilt her into an almost entirely new boat.

Osborne also is said to have employed *Sea Dart* as the set of a television program for children. Searches in British television archives have not uncovered such a program or even a segment within a program.

Any television appearance may have been a one-time show, a limited run, an appearance on a single episode of a children's show; or maybe the story is just another wisp of fog.

The story continues that at the conclusion of the television program or series, 'Captain' Osborne literally sailed *Sea Dart* into the sunset, on a voyage that was supposed to continue around the world.

Sea Dart's departure was noted by *The Times* of London on August 26, 1970. (Oddly, the Romsey newspaper appears not to have written about it.) Peace talks were beginning in the Middle East; the Charles Manson trial, which dominated U.S. papers at the time, was a short article on page 5. On page 10, *Sea Dart's* sailing was overshadowed by that of two men aged 81 and 68 who sailed to the Bahamas in a larger boat: "Age no bar on yacht trip to Bahamas," the headline says. A separate paragraph, following the main article, reads:

> Mrs. Doreen Osborne, aged 29, left the Isles of Scilly yesterday with her husband Jim, aged 29, on a round-the-world trip in a 21-foot sailing boat named *Sea Dart*. They sold their home in Romsey, Hampshire, and their car to buy the bare hull of the boat and fit it for a journey they estimate will take two years.

This is the only mention to date discovered of *Sea Dart's* voyage. It is also the first, and so far only, reference to Doreen Osborne.

What happened between August 1970 and March 1971, between the Isles of Scilly and the island of Barbados, the easternmost point in the West Indies? After all their planning and hard work, Jim and Doreen may have run into trouble in the close confines of *Sea Dart's* cabin. They would not be the first couple to find that the day-to-day reality of ocean voyaging was more togetherness than they really wanted to enjoy.

But what became of Doreen? Did she jump ship at the first landfall and fly back home? Or start a new life somewhere between England and the West Indies? Was she washed overboard, losing her footing on the rounded deck? Or, one wonders darkly, might she have been *pushed*? Until replies come in from friends, neighbors or Doreen herself, the possibilities are endless and intriguing.

In any case, James Osborne apparently was alone on Barbados. After all the hard work and the Atlantic passage he had shared with Doreen and *Sea Dart*, he may simply have not wanted to sail on alone. And like many a young, recently unmarried man, he found the easy-going life of the islands — and the fine local rum — suited him fine. He put *Sea Dart* up for sale at the Barbados Yacht Club.

According to *Sea Dart's* next owner, Osborne stayed at the club, in one of the rooms provided for visiting yachtsmen, until he was thrown out for 'dirty living', something of an accomplishment in free-spirited Barbados.

II. About *Sea Dart's* Registration

Registering a boat is somewhat like obtaining a passport for it. Registration identifies the boat by name and nationality, and shows ownership. In the United Kingdom an owner, who must be a British subject or established resident, will register a boat if he intends to sail beyond the waters of the U.K., or wishes to fly the Red Ensign on a boat more than 24 meters long (identifying the boat as British), or to register a mortgage on the boat.

For registration purposes, a boat consists of 64 shares. (Mark Rice said Jones told him that he, Jones, owned 64 shares "and the rest belongs to England" — but 64 shares *are* the whole boat.)

A person or company may own all the shares, or as little as a fifth of a share if there are many joint owners. *Sea Dart's* registration shows James Frank Bernard Osborne as the owner of all 64 shares. There is no mention of Doreen.

The person registering a boat may choose any of 114 cities as the 'port of choice' with which the boat will be associated. Nowhere do the regulations say that the boat ever has to sail from that port, though that would be logical, and most boats probably are registered at a port close to home. Osborne registered *Sea Dart* at Southampton, the major seaport close to Romsey.

Sea Dart was registered in the United Kingdom in 1965. A certificate of registry at that time was issued 'for eternity', or until the vessel no longer met the registration criteria. Officially, then, 'eternity' ended for *Sea Dart* in 1972. The last note on the transcript of registration says, "Registry closed and Certificate of Registry cancelled this 8th day of March 1972 on sale of vessel to a foreigner (American subject). Advice received from owner."

In a 1989 letter, Tristan Jones said that he hoped *Sea Dart* was flying the Red Ensign. He said she must because she was British, and *Lloyd's Register of Yachts* still listed her as British. Lloyd's Register, the organization, reports no record of *Sea Dart*; she does not appear in any edition of *Lloyd's Register of Yachts* from 1960 to 1980. She is listed in the *Mercantile Navy Lists*, specifically the editions of 1967, 1968 and 1971, under Osborne's ownership.

A "Declaration by Individual Owner or Transferee" stamped by the British Embassy in Montevideo in 1975, shows Tristan Jones as owner of 64 out of 64 shares.

That paper also shows her name as *Sea Dart of Titicaca* and her registry as "1974 Liverpool." Jones, from South America, claimed Liverpool (perhaps because that was where he was registered himself as an infant) as *Sea Dart's* home port. He painted *Liverpool* on her stern, clearly visible in his photographs.

Tristan Jones represented *Sea Dart* as being registered, to the point of declaring her British territory, as if she possessed diplomatic immunity. His declarations, and his later assertion that she *must* wear the British Red Ensign, may have been based on belief, but *not on fact*.

For the Registry of Shipping and Seamen had closed the registry on *Sea Dart* when they received word that she had been sold to an American. Although Jones subsequently filled out a transfer/declaration of ownership, if he ever filed any registration with one of the embassies in South America, it apparently was not forwarded to England.

All this taken together shows clearly that *Sea Dart* was not officially registered in the United Kingdom when Tristan Jones owned her. The register was never re-opened, so she was *not registered at all* after 1972.

Did Tristan Jones know *Sea Dart* was unregistered? From his statements, it appears not. But if he did, then his bluff was better than his readers ever imagined!

Sea Dart sailing in the Caribbean, trim and lively, with dolphins on her bow. PHOTO BY RON REIL. Inset: Ron Reil on Mt Borah, Idaho, 1970s. PHOTO COURTESY OF RON REIL.

III. Sailing the West Indies

Ron Reil, a 24-year-old electronics technician stationed with the U.S. Navy in Barbados, came to look at *Sea Dart* with a friend who was interested in buying the boat. Since the owner wasn't about and they weren't sure which dinghy onshore belonged to her, they swam out to *Sea Dart* to look her over.

Reil still recalls swimming to the boat and coming up under her elegant bowsprit with the hand-carved dolphins that graced her bow. By the time Jim Osborne arrived to show them around, Reil was in love with the beautifully crafted little wooden boat.

Meeting Osborne, he recalls, he estimated the man to be between 35 and 40 years old rather than 29, and quite recently arrived on the island, perhaps only by a couple of weeks. And he is quite certain that Osborne never mentioned a wife. He was busy pursuing every girl within reach, including one or two of Reil's particular friends.

On the drive back to Speightstown, Reil's companion said *Sea Dart* was too much boat for what he had in mind.

"Do you mind if I buy her?" Reil asked. And on April 27, 1971, she was his.

Barbados required that the transaction be conducted in local currency. Reil was paid in U.S. Dollars. When he went to the bank to exchange U.S. $4,250 for $6,500 in local currency, the request raised some eyebrows. The largest denomination, he recalls, was a twenty-dollar bill. The bankers responded with stacks of ones, fives and tens; Reil drove to the capital, Bridgetown, with a backseat full of cash, and took ownership of *Sea Dart*. Once she was his, he sailed her twenty miles up the island to his house on Gibbs Bay, where she joined his larger sloop, *Vega*.

Ron Reil had always lived close to the sea, and he thrived on adventure from an early age. His father, a much-decorated veteran of World War II, was an Air Force officer, so the boy grew up all over. The family lived at various times in Connecticut, Newfoundland, California, Mississippi — and on Okinawa, where the boy read Thor Heyerdahl's adventure classic *Kon-Tiki*, and fell under its spell. There, also, he learned to sail and dive. In the West Indies, as a petty officer second class, Reil describes his duty as being "involved with submarine surveillance, *Hunt for Red October* stuff."

Several months before he found *Sea Dart*, Reil met his hero at sea. Heyerdahl was completing his voyage from Egypt to the Americas on *Ra II*, and when Reil received word of the reed craft approaching the island, he sailed out 24 miles in *Vega* to meet it. *Vega*, he said, was the third boat to reach *Ra II*; the only craft to reach it sooner were two powerboats. (Thor Heyerdahl's article about the crossing for *National Geographic* includes a photo of some of the boats that met *Ra II* off Barbados on July 12, 1970; *Vega* is most likely just out of the picture, to the right.) He sailed alongside and exchanged greetings as best he could with Heyerdahl and the raft's multinational crew. Then *Ra II* continued on, led by a tugboat, to a hero's welcome from the thousands of people waiting in Barbados. Heyerdahl invited Reil to visit later, after the excitement died down, and he explored the craft to his heart's content.

Reil sailed *Sea Dart* in the waters of Barbados and other islands of the West Indies until he had to move on to Norfolk, Virginia, for his final Navy assignment. He watched the Caribbean weather anxiously, and breathed a sigh of relief as each storm bypassed Barbados. At last, in October 1972, he was through with the Navy and free to return to *Sea Dart*. After a quick visit to his family, by then living in Oregon, Reil connected in Florida with his friend Brooks FitzPatrick, who would serve as first mate and cook, and they flew to Barbados.

They found *Sea Dart* in terrible condition. He had left her with people who promised to take care of her in exchange for sailing her; but he found wet, moldy sails in the closed cabin, badly warped decking, brass fittings so corroded by the salt air that they broke off in his hands. Weeks of hard work lay ahead before she could sail again, including a week at the Careenage, the old harbor in Bridgetown where boats have been careened for scraping and painting since boats first arrived on Barbados.

After *Sea Dart* was safely anchored again at Gibbs Bay, the captain of the navy facility asked Reil to take the captain's yacht to the Careenage for similar work. Reil and Fitz were living on sixty cents a day, and the offer of $250 in pay was a fortune to them.

Because the captain's boat lacked an engine and heavy-duty anchors, Reil borrowed the necessary equipment from *Sea Dart*. They sailed the captain's boat to Bridgetown and set to work, staying on the boat to protect it from thievery.

On the afternoon of their third day in Bridgetown, an inter-island freighter was violently pushed backward at the dock, shattering the two-to-three-foot-thick bowsprits on several boats. A similar push was repeated a couple of hours later, but with less damage, since the boats were tied more securely. The ocean on the west, or leeward, side of the island is generally calm and clear, and this day seemed no exception; but Reil felt that all was not well.

That evening a friend called Macky, a long-time resident of the island, arrived from Gibbs Bay with frightening news: *Sea Dart* was in serious danger. The only way to reach her was to motor back to Gibbs Bay and approach from the sea, hoping they would arrive in time. Macky took Reil and Fitz in his 36-foot yacht, *Silver Sprinter*, all sails set and diesel engine working as well, and they raced north.

By the time they reached Gibbs Bay, Reil had realized they were riding huge waves created by a faraway storm or some other disturbance, waves that, as they rose, seemed to tilt the entire sea. And he heard the powerful, low-pitched sound of the surf, a mile shoreward.

Sea Dart was riding the enormous waves, only yards from where they broke against the shore, helpless without an engine. Reil borrowed Macky's dinghy, promised his friend that he wouldn't get killed, and rowed toward *Sea Dart*. Fitz accompanied him to climb aboard *Sea Dart*, pull a 600-foot emergency line out of the lazarette for towing, and lift the anchor.

For a few moments the waves held back.

Fitz paid out as much as he could of the line, while Reil began rowing toward the mouth of the bay. But only some fifty feet of line ran smoothly before Fitz hit a bad tangle and had to cleat off the line. He pulled up the anchor and stayed with *Sea Dart* to steer her. Before the next mountain range of water reached them, Reil rowed with all his strength back toward *Silver Sprinter*, a line held between his knees, and threw the line to Macky as the yacht passed him. There was only one chance to make the catch; and they were successful. The two boats were connected by a single ¾-inch-diameter nylon line, a thread against the enormous waves.

Reil watched from the dinghy in fear, and then in awe, as *Silver Sprinter* pulled *Sea Dart* out toward the waves. The next mountain of water stormed toward shore, lifting *Silver Sprinter* until, at its peak, she was three-quarters out of the water. The line connecting the two boats stretched and thinned to less than half its normal diameter as it cut through the wave. Then *Silver Sprinter* disappeared completely into the trough behind the towering water, and it was *Sea Dart*'s turn to take on the terrifying slope.

She rode the wave, buoyant as she could be, until she in her turn appeared ready to launch into the sky. Then she dropped down the other side, and the two boats were safely on their way to deep water.

The friends learned next day that almost every boat in Gibbs Bay had been damaged — dashed on the shore or shoved into the sand by the huge waves. And Reil had learned his lesson: once the captain's job was completed, he quickly returned *Sea Dart*'s engine and other gear to her, and never risked her safety that way again.

Reil and *Sea Dart* shared many other adventures. There were times when Reil found himself and *Sea Dart* in peril after settling into what seemed to be well-protected anchorages.

Once on the windward side of Palm Island, one of the southernmost of the Grenadines, they sailed into a reef-protected bay that only a shoal-draft boat such as *Sea Dart* could enter. Going ashore, Reil met

Sea Dart hauled out for painting at Gibbs Bay. Her trim and keels are reddish brown. PHOTO BY RON REIL.

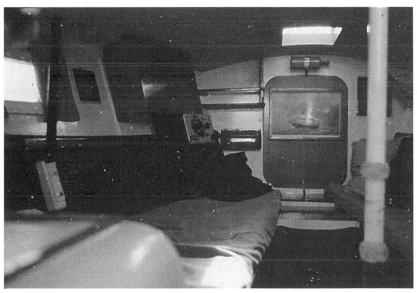

Cabin interior facing forward from the galley. PHOTO BY RON REIL.

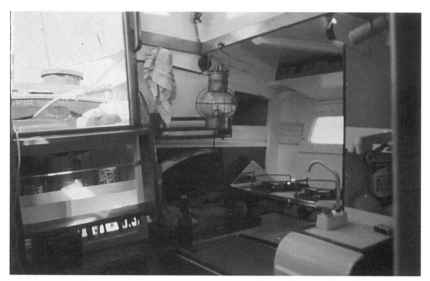

Interior view of the navigation table (left) and the galley with its sink and the gimballed stove and lanterns. Photo by Tristan Jones.

sailing writer John Caldwell, author of *Desperate Voyage*. That night, *Sea Dart* was trapped in the bay by big, rolling waves and bounced about by a four-foot chop. Pulling the anchor at first light, Reil and Fitz sailed out of the bay over a reef that seemed much shallower than it had the day before. Suddenly a wave rose up, sheer as a cliff in front of them. *Sea Dart* "punched a hole in it," Reil says, sailing on through the wave and out to deep water.

A little north of Palm Island is a cluster called Tobago Cays, where Reil and Fitz anchored one day and Reil went diving for his dinner, as was his custom. The area had been fished out, but he thought he might find some conchs, whose rich meat was an occasional treat. Swimming about 150 yards from *Sea Dart*, he saw a school of tuna in the distance. When a fish broke from the school and came toward him, he shot it with his air-powered spear gun and held on as the tuna swam, towing him behind, wrapping his line around the corals. At last, the fish nosed down and lay dead on the bottom, and Reil was overjoyed. Bringing in a 200-pound tuna meant plenty of food for him and Fitz, with enough left over to sell to people on the other boats in the harbor.

A shark appeared out of nowhere, grabbed the front half of the tuna in one bite and swam away, shaking and eating the hundred-pound half-fish. And as Reil watched, helpless, a *second* shark swam in and seized the other half of the tuna.

The diver returned to the surface with no fish at all, to find that a crowd of people up above had watched the whole strange performance.

One night as Reil and Fitz sailed north of the island of St. Vincent, a pod of humpback whales passed by *Sea Dart*. One whale came toward the boat.

"It scared about 10 years' life out of me," Reil recalls. "I thought she was coming right through the side. Another yacht had been sunk that way about a year earlier, and I knew the story well." But this whale passed below *Sea Dart*, just under her keels. Reil called to Fitz, but the whales were gone in a brief moment.

"She was really easy to see in the dark water," Reil said, "because she was completely outlined by the glowing plankton as she came at us and passed under."

Reil and Fitz sailed *Sea Dart* to the island of Bequia, the northernmost and largest of the Grenadines in the long curve of islands south of St. Vincent, in early 1973. Bequia was a friendly island, where the main local occupations at that time were boatbuilding and nineteenth-century-style whaling. It was the only place remaining where men still went on 'Nantucket sleigh rides' to hunt humpback whales. And it was an easy place to stay. The young Americans could dive for their dinner, enjoy a party on a different yacht every evening, and body surf only a few miles away on the far side of the island.

But here Fitz and Reil came to a parting of the ways. Though they were good friends, they differed in their approach to the seagoing life. Reil enjoyed sailing in all conditions, as well as the partying and the various other pleasures of the islands. Fitz was devoutly religious, a teetotaller; he also got seasick when the water was rough. On March 1, Fitz left for home.

Reil, saying farewell to his friend and to a promising romance with an island lady, found single-handed sailing not to his taste and the burdens of live-aboard boat ownership heavy. He decided he would sell *Sea Dart.*

Shortly after Fitz left, Reil encountered Tristan Jones for the first time.

Jones had just sailed into Bequia on *Banjo II.* He had acquired *Banjo* as a fill-in after returning *Barbara,* the yawl he had taken to the Dead Sea, around Africa and up the Amazon, to her owner in the United States.

"My first glimpse of Tristan," Reil recalls, "occurred one early morning when I was brought to *Sea Dart*'s deck by a big ruckus ashore. High up on the hill, in town, I could see Tristan running down the road toward the bay, as fast as he could go, with the local sailmaker right behind him waving a big machete and screaming profanities at him. Apparently Tristan had pulled a fast one on the sailmaker and was about to pay for it with his life.

"Tristan was fleet of foot, however, and reached the end of the town dock about three steps ahead of the sailmaker's machete. Tristan launched off the dock gracefully, clearing 20 feet of water before entering the sea in a headlong dive. He swam out to *Banjo* and climbed aboard in a fierce temper. He could be heard all over the bay cussing at his two young black crewmen. It has been said that Tristan couldn't swim, but . . . I think he must have forgotten that fact for a moment."

Reil saw Jones frequently over the next several days, though Jones kept to his own boat and did not join in the harbor parties.

"Tristan loved the rum bottle," Reil recalls, "especially someone else's rum bottle, and would often come back to *Banjo* in a fierce roaring mood that would get the whole bay up on deck to watch."

On one occasion, when his crew didn't pick him up in the dinghy, Reil says Jones waded into the water, once again forgot he couldn't swim, and climbed aboard *Banjo* in a temper. He stormed below, returned with one of his young crewmen held aloft and tossed him into the sea, then brought up the second one. When they climbed aboard, he had not yet cooled down, so he threw them in again, while everyone in the bay watched his display of fury.

Jones had learned that Reil wanted to sell *Sea Dart* and hailed him from shore one day to discuss a possible deal. Reil was sure that Jones had not heard of the boat before arriving; but Jones wrote in *The Incredible Voyage* that he had heard mention of her on another island and had looked for her all over the Caribbean.

Jones' account is concise, and quite simple: he wrote that he saw *Sea Dart* and, after locating the owner, completed the purchase two days later. He wrote that he paid about $U.S. 5,000 for the boat.

Reil recalls the transaction somewhat differently. He says that he picked up Jones in *Sea Dart's* dinghy, and they negotiated the sale that afternoon and evening over a gallon-and-a-half jug of rum. The purchase price was about $U.S. 3,500, plus a couple of hundred or so for the instruments Jones insisted on getting with the boat. Once this was settled, Reil chose to keep *Sea Dart* until April 1, so he could cruise through the Grenadines one last time.

But shortly after they came to terms, the perils of single-handed sailing struck Reil with force: a spider bit him on the back of his right calf.

"It turned out to be very poisonous," he recalls, "and soon the wound was a horrible mass of rotting flesh. Nothing I did made any difference." Swollen, painful and situated where he couldn't reach it well himself, the bite resisted all his self-medication efforts, even sea water, his lifelong cure for every ill. And there was little or no medical help available in Bequia.

Fortunately, into port sailed a British couple he knew, Neil and Hilary Sanders. Hilary examined the wound with a magnifying glass and a sharp knife, and discovered seven distinct cores in its center.

While Reil fought to concentrate on a bottle of rum and his conversation with Neil, Hilary opened the festering sore, carved out the cores of the bite, packed it with sulfa powder and expertly bandaged it. The wound healed quickly. "Within three days I was back in the sea diving for my dinner again," Reil recalls. "It was a tremendous load off my shoulders to know I was not going to die."

Once he was well again, Reil remembered he had great news for them — the sale of *Sea Dart*. He was deeply disturbed to learn that Tristan Jones had earlier agreed to buy *their* boat. Like him, they had decided to sail one more time through the Grenadines before turning over the boat; and while they were gone, Jones had located (or discovered) *Sea Dart*, which was better suited to the voyage he planned.

Checking at the bank, they learned Jones had told the banker they had cancelled the agreement, gotten his deposit money back, and put it down on *Sea Dart*. They insisted that Reil continue with his sale, and soon sailed out of the harbor. (Twenty-five years later Reil learned that Neil and Hilary never left Bequia. With their money gone, unable to return to England, they found jobs on the island and made their home there.)

This episode severely strained relations between Reil and Jones, who were spending considerable time together as they prepared to switch boats. The tension eased somewhat after Neil and Hilary left, and Reil agreed to skipper *Banjo* back to the States for her new owners, an American couple.

Then one day Reil went body surfing on the other side of the island with some friends. He returned to discover that Jones had come aboard *Sea Dart*, searched out her log and left a note saying he would sue if Reil told anyone the unpleasant details of the boat sale.

"He was very concerned about his image to his readers," Reil said. "This was quite a shock to me considering that everything in the log was a strict record of all events as they happened, with only occasional personal comments or observations."

The result was another go-round and Reil considered canceling the sale. But they went forward with the plan, and on April 1, 1973, *Sea Dart* became the property of Tristan Jones. The boats were rafted together and the sailors transferred their belongings, Reil to much larger quarters on *Banjo* and Jones to the smaller space available on *Sea Dart*.

"At one point there was a big pile of stuff in *Banjo*'s cockpit waiting to be tossed over the side," Reil says. "On the pile was an old world atlas. I picked it up, looked through it, and was amazed to see that every page that had ocean on it had dozens of red and blue pencil lines drawn in. They were all the various routes Tristan had sailed over the years. It was a testament to a man's solitary life at sea, and to an enormous number of miles at sea. He had sailed just about every place that could be sailed between the Arctic and Antarctic oceans, and then some. I really regret throwing the book back on the pile, as it was a monument to a really amazing life, no matter what Tristan and I thought of each other."

And regardless of their conflicts, Reil recalls that Jones was a spellbinding storyteller. During those evenings of the transition between boats, with the rum bottle at hand, Jones started talking and Reil listened for hours, enthralled.

Reil dismissed Jones' crew, since he did not need their help and could not afford to feed them. The boys soon found employment on a bare-boat charter where their sailing skills were needed, and sailed away. Reil prepared *Banjo* to sail north with her new owners.

The couple wanted to take an island-hopping route instead of sailing directly to New York. The choice nearly cost them their lives. They had to go through a dangerous stretch off the island of Hispaniola (Dominican Republic and Haiti), where Haitian pirates came alongside holding big machetes hidden where their intended victims would not see them until too late. Reil was prepared. He pulled out his double-barreled shotgun and held the barrels close to the pirate leader's forehead. The pirate and his crew smiled and backed down.

Only hours later, *Banjo* was caught in a hurricane; she capsized and nearly sank. When they arrived in Florida, the new owners put the boat up for sale and went home — by air.

Reil went out to Oregon and studied geology and engineering. After years of field work and further adventures that included climbing live volcanoes, he became a teacher. Today, he explains the workings of ocean currents and volcanic eruptions to his earth sciences classes through his stories and the slides he has taken while diving, spelunking and sailing. His students pay attention.

Sea Dart and *Banjo II* rafted together at Bequia, as Ron Reil and Tristan Jones prepare to trade boats. PHOTO BY RON REIL.

Tristan Jones writing magazine articles in the cabin of *Sea Dart.* PHOTO BY TRISTAN JONES.

IV. Tristan Jones

Ron Reil noted in his log, at the time he sold her to Jones, that in a few months *Sea Dart* would be famous. And so she was.

And why?

Because she crossed South America — and because Tristan Jones told her story.

The voyage alone would have made *Sea Dart* a celebrity. Jones' telling of the tale has given her an enduring fame.

In *The Incredible Voyage*, as in the books that followed it, there is a story worth telling. That, however, is only the beginning. For beyond and above the story itself is the *way* he tells that story. His words roll and crash like the waves he describes, conveying moods and thoughts as directly as if he were speaking to the reader across a pub table.

Reading *The Incredible Voyage* is a painful journey for reader as well as writer, the long miles at sea stretching out before you and the jungle pressing in until you nearly pass out in the hot, writhing green hell he describes. It takes little imagination to *feel*, not just *see*, how it was to curl up in *Sea Dart*'s tiny cabin, surrounded by gear, trying to sleep with giant moths beating at the hatchway.

Some articles about Tristan Jones are filled with "he claims" and "he says" as the writers list his voyages and travels, if for no other reason than that some of the feats he claimed defy belief. This account will follow that practice to some extent, simply because there is no other verifying statement available. British embassies along his route, for example, keep all their records private for thirty years, never release information from the consular section, and forbid their personnel to discuss individual cases. Records at other agencies, companies and organizations have long since been destroyed or placed deep in archives, inaccessible for all practical purposes.

Yet the customs logs and registers at ports around the world bear record that he was there when he said he was.

He was, at least in those cases, where he said he was, when he said he was there. That much can be verified. What happened between those points, the objective truthfulness of his accounts, is between him and God. Perhaps he sacrificed fact for some truth he saw beyond the facts. Perhaps he believed, literally, every word he put on paper, at least at the time. Perhaps some of what he recorded was the product of sleep deprivation, malnutrition and solitude.

Whatever the facts, Tristan Jones was a masterful storyteller. No one would argue that. When Jones had an audience, said Tom Thornton of Andrews & McMeel, he would embellish as he went along until the tale "ended up a fish story." But, Thornton continued, "I think he was credible in his writing," where the temptation to play to an audience was reduced.

In some of his books Jones admitted changing names of people and ships "to save embarrassment to relatives" or other people. He made no such disclaimer in *The Incredible Voyage*, but since he didn't introduce people by saying "I met a sailor I will call Albert," it is hard to tell whether he identified people or boats by their real names. Since much of his sailing was single-handed, he's the only one who would know the facts of a given voyage. And he wouldn't be the first writer to create composite "characters" — in this case, ships or events — or heighten the drama of an adventure to spin a better story than the logbook provides.

"I sail a lot," Greg Allen of Seattle said — and he speaks for many sailors — "and I know a lot of people who sail a lot, and all of us put together haven't had as many adventures as Tristan Jones. You go out, you sail from point A to point B, you have good weather, good company, a pleasant, uneventful trip."

But there is a difference. First, none of the people he's sailing with is Tristan Jones. None of them is as determined as Jones to reach a given point by a given date, so much so that he'll sail hundreds of miles on tack after tack against one of the most powerful currents on earth. None of them is as obsessed with his own seafaring vision of man contesting nature, a concept of struggle, survival and above all endurance: in the poet's phrase, "to strive, to seek, to find and not to yield." And none of them is likely, even if he can, to transform on paper a squall into a storm or a brief encounter with a customs official into a rage against the whole world of officialdom — one of Jones' lifelong battles.

Even if "one did have to take some of the things he wrote with a couple tons of salt," as one writer observed, the stories he wove from his logbooks and reminiscences, and a nimble imagination, continue to fascinate readers all over the world.

What appears to be fact in Tristan Jones' life story is fantastical enough for a shelf of novels.

Tristan Jones literally was born at sea on May 8, 1924, aboard the ship *Western Star* (or *Star of the West*: biographical notes give the name both ways) near the island of Tristan da Cunha in the South Atlantic, nearly midway between the capes of Horn and Good Hope. It was that island for which he was named. It was a fitting start for a life that would be lived more — and more fully — at sea than on land.

The ship was bound for Halifax, Nova Scotia, and if she had landed there, he would have had British citizenship because of his parents and Canadian citizenship for the first part of the British Empire that the ship touched. But the owners sent a radio message redirecting the ship to their home port, Liverpool; so the baby was doubly a British subject.

This beginning was also fitting for a sailor-in-the-making who traced his family's affinity with the sea at least to a great-great-great-great-grandfather, William Jones of Beddgelert, master of the brig *Harlech Castle*, which was at St. Petersburg, Russia, in 1795.

According to his recollections in *A Steady Trade* and *Heart of Oak*, Tristan lived with his mother, father and sister Angharad in the small

Welsh coastal hamlet of Llangareth (Llanarth). "A chapel, three cottages and our house," is how he describes it, "nestled, chimneys smoking, hidden in a little valley so green that the golden rocky outcrops of the Ffestiniog mountains looked from the heights to us children like the claws of an eagle outsplayed on well-brushed green baize."

According to his own account he was raised in an atmosphere of hard work, unsentimental affection, homegrown food and a fierce loyalty to family and place. He was Welsh to the core, allowing the word 'British' to describe him but rarely the term 'English'. Welsh was his first language at home; English he learned at school, along with an English-slanted view of history. The legends he treasured were taught in Welsh by storytellers who rolled the words out in time-honored cadences. Like Dylan Thomas, Richard Llewellyn and other Welsh writers, Tristan Jones came to handle English words with a Welsh appreciation that transformed them into fire, or sparkles, or bubbling music. Not just any music, either, but music as sung in the Welsh chapel, four-part harmonies rising rich and full from the whole heart and soul of a congregation.

By the age of thirteen, Jones had already spent a goodly amount of time at sea with local fishermen, earning a share in the catch in fish or cash. And he had been raised on tales of the sea — family stories, Welsh legends, tales from his father's friends. Going to sea was inevitable.

As soon as he could be licensed for work on a boat, Tristan Jones left Wales for an apprenticeship on a coastal sailing barge. He was fourteen. His two years on board were an education in seamanship and the handling of a 95-foot double-masted working craft far larger than most of the boats he would sail in later life. His narrative, *A Steady Trade*, is filled with sea air, sweat and nostalgia for a way of life since disappeared.

At sixteen, lying about his age, he joined the Royal Navy for an enlistment of twelve years (from the age of eighteen — so he was signed up for fourteen years in all). Learning his way around warships, he observed that the stokers in the boiler room had some of what we would call 'down time' between chores, and consequently some of them had leisure for reading. Reading became one of the young seaman's passions, a way to continue his education and connect with minds of the past.

He served on several vessels during World War II, surviving three sinkings before his eighteenth birthday. Both of his parents died during the war; his sister married soon after and moved to the other side of the world. Jones continued in the Navy until he was injured either by a shot or a mine explosion (there are at least two versions of the story) in Aden. He was discharged with a minuscule total-disability pension.

After a short period of self-pity, he resolved to go to sea anyway; if not with the Navy, then on his own, in small boats. He began delivering yachts to make a living, sailing them to various ports around the world for their owners. He may have been 'totally disabled', but nothing could stop him from sailing. He also began writing articles for sailing magazines from England to Australia.

In the late 1950s, he acquired and refitted a lifeboat he called *Cresswell*. Accompanied by a one-eyed, three-legged dog named Nelson, he sailed north in quest of a northern-latitude sailing record. He and Nelson spent more than a year stuck in the floating ice, he wrote later, with everything in the boat iced over for months and a massive berg looming above until it finally crashed and broke the boat free. Then he sailed west, survived a dismasting, drifted with the current and ended up in Norway. In *Ice*, he wrote nearly fifteen years later of the darkness and the lessons he took from this unforgiving school of survival.

Once returned from the arctic, he sailed whenever possible, and worked at Harrods department store in London, where he planned an ambitious new voyage while keeping the store's boilers stoked.

As sailing competitions proliferated in which skippers raced around and around the globe, he said he wanted to seek a record that no one could break: the *vertical* sailing record. He would sail an ocean-going boat on the lowest navigable body of water on earth — the Dead Sea — and the highest — Lake Titicaca. And since he also felt disdain for the commercialism of the record-seeking events, he would make the journey without a sponsor.

Over the years Jones accepted assistance, samples, free equipment and donations of cash, and he acknowledged many gifts in his books; but he made it clear that voyaging under the aegis of any commercial sponsor was not to be considered. In one speech, after he had made numerous such voyages, he commented wryly that astronauts in their government-sponsored high-tech space ventures were considered heroes, while he sailed alone, unsponsored, scraping along financially, and was considered an eccentric or worse.

He gained the use of the yawl *Barbara*, and set out for Israel. The first half of *The Incredible Voyage* details his journey to the Dead Sea and around Africa, then the passage to South America in hope of reaching Titicaca from the Amazon. The second half of the book describes his finding *Sea Dart* and tackling the high-altitude record and the passage across South America.

There followed several years spent mostly ashore, writing the books about the voyages past. *The Incredible Voyage* was his first, and more than a dozen others would follow. Jones also continued to write articles for sailing publications as he had done all along, and to plan for future journeys.

In 1982, as the result of a fall and ensuing gangrene, Jones had to have one leg amputated. But he was determined to sail again, and he did — in a trimaran which he named *Outward Leg*. With a crewman, he took the trimaran from San Diego, California, around through the Panama Canal to Europe, and crossed Europe via the Danube and connecting rivers and canals. They sailed on to the Indian Ocean and ended up in Thailand. (See *The Improbable Voyage* and *Outward Leg*.)

Phuket, Thailand, became his base of operations. From there he sent out his Atlantis Society newsletter, the Atlantis Society consisting mainly of Tristan Jones, his current crew and current boat. The purpose of the society was to promote training and voyaging for physically handicapped people, especially Thai youths. Jones assembled a crew and crossed the Kra Isthmus in Thailand on a fishing boat, the *Henry Wagner*, named for a bookseller in the U.S. who supported Jones' voyages, distributed his newsletter and accepted donations on his behalf.

The Kra crossing of 1987, Jones' last major journey by boat, was detailed in *To Venture Further*. Subsequent planned voyages did not materialize as he had hoped, either for financial or health reasons. In 1991 his other leg was amputated as a result of blood clots after another illness and surgery.

His September, 1991, newsletter was headed "Triumph and Disaster":

"1991: the year of America's triumph, events that I had hopefully anticipated for so long, was my own year, so far, of catastrophe.

"Hospitalized in March for a gut-obstruction, subsequent surgery caused a blood clot in my remaining leg. The clot was removed, and I was discharged from the hospital in late May. But the circulation problem persisted and my right leg was amputated below the knee on September 4th. This leaves me a double amputee. I am slowly recovering from the surgery and composing my spirits so that I may again be useful in some way. My first aim is to survive until the Thai version of my book *To Venture Further* is published (and issued as proposed by the publisher) to all the schools in this country (Thailand). I yet have little energy, but what I have I expend in encouraging others to persist; this helps me to survive.

"My latest book, *To Venture Further*, is published in the U.S.A. by I learst-Morrow.

"Your help is urgently needed to help me pay for my medical treatment, as I was uninsurable. Funds are also needed to help my future work in changing attitudes toward the disabled."

He repeated these themes in other letters. Various readers, friends and fellow sailors contributed toward his expenses. Jones continued to work: he devised a boat that a sailor without legs could launch alone; he gave readings, lectured, tended his Atlantis Society projects, and wrote.

The advent of the Internet and e-mail reduced Jones' isolation, putting him in touch with sailors and readers all over the world. In May 1995, for his seventy-first birthday, one correspondent passed on birthday-greeting postings to him, and he replied:

"Many thanks indeed for your passing on to me the postings. They are a great comfort and encouragement to me. I was well and truly 'stranded' here in 1991. I did my best to set off for the U.S.A. in October 1993, for a trip up the East Coast Intracoastal Waterway, arranged by friends, on a catamaran from the Florida Keys. But I had an attack of (of all things) 'hives'. The canceling of that trip . . . foreboded the end of meetings with Americans in the U.S.A. Then along came news of the Internet, and I literally 'bust a gut' to get on it. It was worthwhile. I am berthed again next to my buddies . . . .

[In response to a comment about his being "a real man, not a figment of imagination"] " . . . unless we seek out reality it's easy nowadays (I suppose it always has been) to live in a world of 'figments'. But as T.S. Eliot said: 'Humanity can accept only so much reality'. My reality now would have been, to me thirty years ago, too awful to contemplate. But thank God I can — not accept it — [but] stare it straight in the eye and try to ease the lot of others who might find themselves in the same pit. It has little to do with generosity or courage on my part. I am privileged to be in this situation, and it saves me expecting someone else to do it. That too, now, would be too awful to contemplate."

He mentioned articles that he had 'on the shelf', available for publication, about boats, sailing, his activities in Thailand. And then he wrote:

"Monday is my birthday. Ten years ago I was in Budapest, Hungary onboard *Outward Leg*. Twenty years ago in Montevideo, Uruguay, onboard *Sea Dart*. Thirty years ago in *Cresswell* at Tangiers, Morocco. Forty years ago between boats in Rio [de Janeiro], Brazil; fifty years ago, on guard duty in a destroyer in the North Sea . . . Sixty years ago out on my first fishing-under-sail trip alone in the Irish Sea. What changes there have been in the world! Imagine if we'd had anything like this thing I'm tapping on sixty years ago! What good luck the young lads and lasses have today! And so they should, too . . . but they should know that sailing is one sure way to learn what reality is . . . "

Tristan Jones died on June 21, 1995, from complications after a stroke. He had logged some 450,000 miles at sea, much of it under sail in small boats. He had published countless articles and some sixteen books, most of them autobiographical. Another collection of reminiscences was published in late 1995. (A full list of his books appears in the appendix.) Through his published tales and informative articles he reached millions of readers around the world and "[shoved] the spirit of sail into places and heads where it has never been," as he once phrased it, inspiring both on-water and armchair sailors with new adventurousness.

V. The Incredible Voyage: Up to the Lake

Tristan Jones sailed *Sea Dart* out of the Bequia harbor on April 10, 1973, bound first for Curaçao as they began their voyage together into history — the adventure that Jones would masterfully describe in *The Incredible Voyage*.

The voyage, as mentioned before, was Jones' second attempt to reach Lake Titicaca. He and a crewman had sailed *Barbara* from the Dead Sea down the east coast of Africa, across the Atlantic and then up the Amazon toward the Andes some 1,400 miles before bowing to the superior force of the mighty river's current. Jones had vowed he would reach his goal no matter what the cost in time and pain. Lake Titicaca had become his personal grail.

Jones used the passage to Curaçao to acquaint himself with *Sea Dart*'s handling. He found that she performed well, and heeled no more than thirty degrees. Part of that stability stemmed from her design and triple keels; and part of it came from his bending her aluminum mast slightly aft to make the mainsail spill the wind sooner and keep the boat from blowing over in the sudden gusts of wind coming from the cold mountains along the coast.

He planned to explore the coast of Colombia until as late as August, cross through the Panama Canal and then tackle the Humboldt Current in September. He might be fighting the current, or sailing with it, on his way to Peru, depending on whether El Niño arrived that year.

Attaching a large genoa to *Sea Dart*'s bowsprit, Jones increased the area of working sail. In Curaçao he bought a three-month supply of canned food, then pressed on, sighting the headland of Cabo de la Aguja and the port of Santa Marta, Colombia, on April 25.

After a night in Santa Marta, Jones set off against the current toward Cartagena, 170 miles away, keeping an eye out for pirates and smugglers. At Cartagena, Jones left *Sea Dart* tied up under guard and took a plane to Bogotá in search of a small outboard engine for her.

In Bogotá, he wrote, he was robbed twice. His wallet was stolen at the airport taxi stand just after he arrived; the next day his travelers' checks, passport and visa were stolen at gunpoint. He spent five days in jail for not having identification, then two days waiting for the transfer of money from England, and returned to Cartagena by train to hoist sail and clear out of the harbor.

Next passage for *Sea Dart* and her skipper was a slow maneuver through the Gulf of Darien that included nightly lightning storms, an anchorage in the San Bernardo Islands and a run to the coast of Panama. The powerful current and a howling rainstorm in the night took them thirty miles south of Jones' intended destination, Punta Escoces (Scots Point).

After a night at anchor in the shallow bay behind the point, Jones received a visit from a Cuna couple who took him to their village. Their Spanish-speaking chief said he had not heard of a fort in the area, but he knew of some old stones and a ditch. Jones' visit to the site convinced him it was Fort Saint Andrew, a Scottish Jacobite settlement established at the end of the seventeenth century and besieged by the Spaniards. The chief also told Jones about the *Cabellos Rojos* (Red-Hairs) on the other side of the coastal mountains. Jones moved *Sea Dart* north to Bahía Caledonia, so he could hike inland in search of the people he believed to be descendants of the Scots for whom the point was named.

One man from the Cuna village stayed with *Sea Dart*; another accompanied Jones into the mountains, where they met the Cabellos

Rojos and stayed in their village overnight, dining on iguana and communicating mostly with sign language. Jones noted that a majority of the villagers had nothing Indian about their appearance. The next day, two Cabellos Rojos men took them by forest trails to the divide of the Sierra de Darien and an easier way down. Returning to *Sea Dart*, Jones found a fleet of Cuna canoes gathered around her, her caretaker fishing from the bow and drying his catch on the rigging. The whole flotilla sailed back to Punta Escoces, and *Sea Dart* anchored once more off the Cuna village.

On June 14, Jones sailed *Sea Dart* toward the San Blas Islands (Las Muletas), a string of 365 islands, many only a mile long, along the Panamanian coast east of Colón. He took his time sailing through the archipelago, anchoring off small islands at night and calling at the larger ones.

He found little evidence of outside influence in the San Blas Islands except a small, informal hotel at the far northern end of the archipelago. Even today, a guidebook warns that while tourists may visit any of the islands they wish, when going to the smaller islands they must bring their own water and make definite arrangements to be picked up, as there is no regular air or boat service to these tiny dots on the sea.

Leaving the islands for the Panamanian coast, Jones anchored in Nombre de Dios Bay, where Sir Francis Drake lies buried in the sea-bed, and stopped at the fishing village of Portobelo.

Sea Dart had sailed 2,098 miles since Bequia. She arrived at the entrance to the Panama Canal on July 9, was measured for passage and then waited at the Cristóbal Yacht Club for her turn to pass through the great locks to the Pacific. She was scheduled to start through on Friday the thirteenth (obviously the authorities made no allowance for superstition), but the passage was postponed until Sunday. Jones said the delay cost him the assistance of some seminarians who had planned to act as line-handlers; so he found a hippie in the yacht club's laundry room who rounded up three other young men to form a line-handling crew.

Taking a yacht through the fifty-mile Panama Canal requires a sheaf of paperwork, a pilot and four line-handlers on the deck. The boat moves into each lock with a number of other boats, rides the water level as it rises and then passes through to the next lock. The three Miraflores locks on the Atlantic side, each 110 feet wide and 1,000 feet long, move the boats up 85 feet in altitude to Gatun Lake, the long, manmade lake which is fed by the Chagres River; and three more, the Pedro Miguel locks, take them down again to the Balboa Channel and the Pacific Ocean.

"So it was that *Sea Dart* became the first vessel ever to sail through the Panama Canal . . . I worked out a grand system for sailing into the locks and fetching up short with no problem. The four giant hippies lined up across the tiny deck amidships acted as a sail. When we got halfway into the locks, I shouted, 'Down!' and they dropped prone on the deck, and there we were, automatically reefed down . . . By this means, I had enough speed to turn the boat right around into the wind and bring her to a complete stop right in the middle of the lock. Then the line-handlers cast the long lines ashore and the dock-workers walked the boat down, stern first, to the end of the lock." The wind stayed with them through the crossing. Jones' next port of call was the Balboa Yacht Club on the Pacific coast of Panama.

Years later, Jones said he had encountered one of those hippies again at a boatshow. It turned out that the young man had become a doctor and was working at the very hospital where Jones' leg had been removed.

Taboga Island, off the Panamanian coast, became Jones' preparation site for the next stage of the journey. An eight-foot tide, combined with a flat and sandy beach, meant that *Sea Dart* could sit out of the water for several hours at a time and stand on her three keels for cleaning and painting. Jones traveled back and forth by ferry to the mainland for supplies. He cleaned and repainted *Sea Dart*'s bottom with antifouling paint, painted the sides blue-gray to blend with the horizon (a precaution against pirates), repaired sails, sorted and stowed his gear, and laid in a five-month supply of canned goods against the possibility of being forced far out into the Pacific by the current.

The Humboldt Current, the powerful prevailing pattern of the ocean's movement off South America, is a major force for a voyager to reckon with. This is the cold current that carried Thor Heyerdahl's raft *Kon-Tiki* up the coast of South America and pushed it onward to Polynesia, about a hundred-day journey. Misjudging the current, or finding that *Sea Dart* was too small and slow to fight it, would likely send Jones west four thousand miles to the Tuamotu Archipelago in the South Pacific, just like Heyerdahl. In that event, since Polynesia wasn't what *he* had in mind, he would have to come round the southeast part of the ocean and approach Peru with the current, from the south. This was a ten-thousand-mile detour that Jones estimated would mean six months of hard sailing and a year's delay in reaching Lake Titicaca.

Jones calculated the direct distance from Taboga to Callao, Peru, at roughly 1,700 miles; the sailing distance, with *Sea Dart* tacking, at about 3,500. He figured the current would slacken in early September. Nine weeks' sailing would bring them to Callao in mid-November, with six weeks remaining to reach the high lake by the end of the year.

After what he saw as his defeat on the Amazon, the voyage that had begun as a gesture to point out the absurdity of record-setting and ocean cruising competition had become "a deadly serious matter — *a pilgrimage to my pride!*" (Italics are his.)

By September 8, *Sea Dart* was ready and stocked for the voyage with food, kerosene, first-aid gear, charts, material for repairs to sails and rigging, and even, at last, a four-horsepower outboard engine and a gallon of gasoline. And on September 9, Jones weighed anchor and sailed the 37 miles to Pedro González, a small island in the Perlas Group in the middle of the Gulf of Panama, where he spent his last Panamanian money drinking beer at the shanty-store, surrounded by bags of rice, tobacco, kerosene and fishing gear.

On September 10 he headed *Sea Dart* on her course to Callao, Peru, sailing into winds from the south. He caught sharks, dorado, grouper and swordfish to eat, although the seas became so high he found cooking difficult and ate some of the fish raw. He also pickled some fish in lemon juice to make a rough version of the Caribbean specialty *ceviche*.

Sailing through heavy rain, into light winds and against strong currents, *Sea Dart* made only 600 miles south of Balboa in the first twenty days of the voyage. And on the night of September 29, she met with near-disaster.

Jones had set her to self-steer on a southwesterly tack, close-hauled into a southerly wind. At about 2 a.m., he was thrown from his berth to the roof of the cabin as *Sea Dart* turned upside down, stern over bow — and just as suddenly righted herself, her bowsprit torn from the deck and banging about topside. She had collided with a whale, a tree trunk or something similar, something solid enough to trip her and snap the inch-thick, six-inch-long bolts that secured her handsome bowsprit, leaving a sizeable hole in her marine-ply deck.

Lashing himself to the forward cleats, he sat on the bow to lower the mainsail as the genoa flailed, the bowsprit bumping around at its foot, and rigged a small trysail on the boom to keep *Sea Dart* headed into the wind. After pumping her out with a hand bilge pump, he rigged a makeshift bowsprit by lashing the sprit through the hole in the deck to the ringbolt designed to hold the anchor chain, with the line around the jib-sheet winch and another line securing the middle of the bowsprit to the pulpit stanchions. Then he stuffed sails and shirts into the hole and nailed a canvas patch over it.

He had to put in somewhere for repairs. He knew that some Colombian coastal ports were notorious as drug-smuggling centers, some posed sailing hazards, and others offered an uncertain reception for outsiders. The Perlas Islands and Ecuador were too far away. The remaining option, if it even existed, was the small Colombian island called Gorgona where, rumor said, political prisoners were exiled and from which they did not return.

After two hard nights and a day, *Sea Dart* arrived on the lee side of Gorgona and was greeted almost at once by guards who informed Jones he could stay twenty-four hours, they would not provide food or water, and he was not to speak to any of the prisoners. He managed the loan of a prisoner to help with his repair work, and permission to pass instructions to the man.

He made a permanent repair for the bowsprit, cutting a patch for the deck and a pad to go underneath it and hold the bolts in place, with a patch of inch-thick mahogany in the ceiling of the forepeak.

The next day, October 3, his borrowed prisoner arrived to help with the bolts. Sending his guard to the seaward side of the boat with a bottle of whisky, Jones signaled to the man that he could speak. The prisoner's tale confirmed rumors of political prisoners held without trial under brutal conditions and with no link to the outside world. The work done, prisoner and guard returned to the island. As Jones sailed away in the late afternoon, he lighted his anchor lamp as a beacon for the prisoners ashore.

Twenty-eight days later, *Sea Dart* arrived in Salinas, Ecuador, for a fresh supply of drinking water. Tacking twenty miles toward shore, then twenty miles away, and standing well offshore at night to avoid uncharted hazards, *Sea Dart* had covered some fifty miles per twenty-four hours through the water, but only an average of seventeen miles in twenty-four hours on the map. Often Jones would find that after sailing all night, he was farther north than he had been at dusk, thanks to the power of the Humboldt Current! And the current was stronger as he neared the equator. Between Gorgona and Salinas, by the taffrail log, *Sea Dart* sailed 1,408 miles, but moved only 240 miles directly south!

Jones said he traveled in the company of seals, walruses and pelicans for days along the shores of this Humboldt-chilled region near the equator. (Galápagos fur seals or southern fur seals might have strayed into those waters, but a walrus would have been very far from home indeed.)

On this coast, although skies are overcast and fog, which is formed as the cold water from Antarctica evaporates in the hot equatorial sun, covers the sea until late afternoon, rain is so rare as to be beyond living memory. The fog and the great swells of the Pacific made sailing these waters hard, exhausting work, and Jones often had to eat his food raw.

Salinas, where he arrived fifty days after leaving Pedro Gonzáles, was Jones' halfway mark to Callao. He had to reach Callao by the end of the year, or wait for the next dry season in the Andes to haul *Sea Dart* up the mountains.

He left *Sea Dart* anchored in front of the harbormaster's office while he went inland to Quito. His entry into and exit from Ecuador, only three days apart, resulted in another altercation with officialdom. This time, he said, the immigration official insisted he pay a $100 entry fee, regardless of his intention to stay such a short time. He didn't pay it on entry, but the official said he could not leave the country without paying. Jones sailed out of Salinas with full water tanks, but $100 poorer.

The voyage from Salinas to Callao required a total of forty-eight days, with *Sea Dart* sailing two thousand miles to cover the seven hundred miles between the two points.

Again, some days the current pushed *Sea Dart* farther north than she had been the day before. Again, the sun was obscured by fog, denying the sailor an opportunity to take sights and work out his position. Again and again, he was tempted to give up, to head out across the Pacific toward warmer, sunnier places and leave the cold, gray, swift current behind. But always the memory of the Amazon, the defeat that he took so personally, came to mind and steeled him to resume his fight against the current.

The winds weakened as he sailed south, so Jones steered *Sea Dart* by hand for the last 300 miles to Callao. Day after day, night after night, with occasional breaks when the wind rose enough to allow the self-steering gear to function, he held her on her course. When he saw a calm coming, he worked inshore to a shallow area to wait for the wind.

During one calm, he woke to find a gigantic, bright red creature (he refers to it both as a jellyfish and as a ray), which he estimated as 25 feet wide, floating under *Sea Dart's* keels, apparently trying to lift the boat. He rapidly hauled in the anchor chain and *Sea Dart* slid over the animal and out to sea.

At last, on December 24, *Sea Dart* arrived at the port of Callao. Since the Red Sea, Tristan Jones had traveled 40,000 miles at sea in the course of his incredible voyage. *Sea Dart*, tiny and already battered, had traveled about 6,000 miles with him.

Neither of them knew it, but her days on the open sea were over.

Sea Dart spent Christmas Eve 1973 on the jetty at Callao, hauled out by crane for a bottom scraping and a coat of antifouling paint, while her skipper dined at the yacht club. There, he said, three of his fellow guests offered to purchase *Sea Dart*, apparently hoping to transfer some of their money out of the country. He was met with interest in his plan to haul her up to Lake Titicaca, and pessimism about his chances for official cooperation since he was a 'gringo'.

On Christmas Day, Jones wrote, he attended a party in Lima. The diplomats in attendance agreed that his trip to Lake Titicaca was impossible both physically and politically without six months' work and considerable bribe money to acquire all the necessary official permissions — neither of which he could afford. An embassy driver returned him to the Callao waterfront. He walked back toward *Sea Dart*, his discouragement deepening with every step in the heavy midsummer heat, until a small bar beckoned irresistibly, and he strode through its swinging doors.

Several bottles of beer later, as the little bar took on the glow of an English pub in the sailor's imagination, an unlikely Father Christmas arrived: a Quechua Indian truck driver Jones called Salomon who was drinking up his money before returning home — to Puno, on the shore of Lake Titicaca!

Salomon and Jones struck a deal for the transport of *Sea Dart*, and Salomon assured Jones there was no need to worry about official papers: he had a brother-in-law in the port authority. Then they caroused through Christmas night.

Note: This account and these dates are based on Jones' published narrative. A reporter who consulted the *Sea Dart* logbook several years later cited entries indicating that Jones left Callao on January 2, 1974, and lowered *Sea Dart* into Lake Titicaca on January 12, 1974.

Salomon arrived the next morning with a weathered Ford flatbed truck a good twenty years old, and dilapidated by hard driving under mountain conditions. It was not a promising sight. But it was a way to carry *Sea Dart* up the mountains, to smuggle her, as it were, through Peru.

So *Sea Dart* became an outlaw.

Recruiting help and a hand crane at the Yacht Club, they hoisted *Sea Dart* from the jetty and lowered her onto the truck bed. The truck's side panels stood about rub-rail height. With her mast unstepped, *Sea Dart* rose just above the sides. She might be visible, but she was nestled safely into her spot, especially when Jones wedged old automobile tires between *Sea Dart* and the sides of the truck, and nailed wooden battens to help hold the keels in place. (Note: While Jones carefully describes the arrangement as placing *Sea Dart* on the truck bed with her bowsprit hanging over the cab, photographs show her bow pointing to the rear, with the cockpit a broom's length from the truck cab.) On the bow he rigged the British Red Ensign and Peruvian courtesy flags. Jones rode in *Sea Dart*'s cockpit, with a broom to knock on the truck cab if they were headed into something too low to clear. Salomon and his female companion rode, and slept, in the truck.

They threaded their way through the streets of Lima, the capital, with flags flying and a policeman holding back traffic for them. They followed the Pan-American Highway across the foggy coastal desert to the port of Pisco and the colonial city of Ica, drove through the night and reached Arequipa, 7,500 feet above the sea, by dusk on the second day. They parked in the main square, hidden in plain sight from police and customs officials.

They awoke to find themselves surrounded by armed policemen and a crowd of curious people. Soon the mayor arrived, spoke at length, and asked what they needed. Jones requested old tractor tires; in minutes they had six of them cushioning *Sea Dart* from the shocks to come on her ride through the Andes. After an evening of celebration, they left Arequipa at midnight to climb the mountains.

There was no time to waste: the rains might have — should have — already started, the snow melting to wash away the mountains and feed the rivers on the west side, and to build the torrent of the Amazon on the east side of the range. Landslides would destroy the road, cutting off surface travel to and from the Puna Altiplano, the high mountain valleys, for four months.

They climbed slowly into the darkness, scaling the wall of the Andes by means of a road, or more accurately, a shelf, which Jones described as no more than 12 feet wide, cut into the cliffside with an edge that dropped away thousands of feet, and *Sea Dart* tilting at a 20-degree angle toward that edge.

By dawn they were on Paso Cimbral at an altitude of 4,300 meters (about 13,000 feet), slowly making their way across a wind-and-rain-worn surface of bare rock, with a drop of a mile or more on one side and a rushing river on the other.

The low Pati tunnel, which had ruled out *Barbara* as the boat for the voyage, loomed in front of them at midday. Even with tires deflated, going through the tunnel was a near scrape; but they got through.

After their second slow, agonizing night on this narrow road, they found themselves in Quechua country, where the people wore ponchos and *chorros* (pointed caps with earflaps), both expertly fashioned from llama wool, and went barefoot in the snow as they tended their llama flocks.

A heavy rainstorm stopped them one evening, and they huddled overnight in *Sea Dart's* tiny cabin. When they got under way again, Salomon's girlfriend and Jones walked ahead of the truck to test the solidity of the road, covering a whole 25 miles that day.

The last day of their ascent, the drying ground let them move forward at about 10 miles per hour. Once they reached Cuzco and the straight road to the lake, they doubled their pace.

The sky was clear and the moon almost full as they arrived in Puno, truck and travelers covered with mud.

"For one unforgettable moment on the way into the town," Jones recalled, "I glimpsed the moon shining on Lake Titicaca. It was calm, inviting, welcoming. Unbelievable — I'd made it! . . . Whatever might happen, I'd made my destination. Almost, for we decided to spend the night in the main square, surrounded by a gaping crowd of Quechua Indians . . .

"I had a lot of trouble getting to sleep in *Sea Dart's* cabin. It wasn't Salomon's snoring, it wasn't the lack of oxygen at almost thirteen thousand feet above sea level; it was out of thankfulness to all the Gods of the Oceans for my arrival at my destination after so long."

Lake Titicaca, at 12,506 feet above sea level, besides being the highest navigable lake in the world, is also the second largest lake in South America after Venezuela's Lake Maracaibo, covering 3,200 square miles. A few lakes in South America and in the Himalayas are situated higher, but they are not considered accessible for navigation.

The lake is at the heart of Andean legend and the tales of the Inca civilization. The name Titicaca is Quechua, derived from the 'rock of the puma', a name which originally applied to the sacred rock, Titi-kala, on the Island of the Sun (Isla del Sol), with the word *kaka* (rock) being substituted for *kala* (stone). The puma or *titi* was a wild black cat of the region, seldom seen but believed to have amazing powers.

Photographs taken from space, published in the *National Geographic* of February 1971, show a startling image: the larger portion of

Sea Dart at 14,800 feet above sea level, with Misti Volcano in the background, being smuggled across Peru on the flatbed of Salomon's ancient Ford truck. PHOTO BY TRISTAN JONES.

The first photo of an ocean-going vessel taken from behind a llama. *Sea Dart* sailing on Lake Titicaca at 12,506 feet above sea level. PHOTO BY TRISTAN JONES.

the lake is easily seen as a great puma, ready to pounce, pursuing a rabbit — the smaller end of the lake.

The two sections, Lago Chucuito and Lago Huinaymarca, are separated by the narrow Strait of Tiquina, a channel about three-quarters of a mile wide which is said to have been formed after the death of the legendary white, bearded Tunupa, 'The Wise One'. His funeral balsa raft swept down to the end of the lake, parted the land, and ran on down to the sea.

This is where the white, bearded Kon-Tiki-Vira-Cocha created the sun, moon and stars after a long period of darkness. This is where the Inca civilization rose to leave its dramatic mark on South American architecture, art and government.

The most important place on the lake is the Island of the Sun, with its temple and sacred rock. Nearby is the Island of the Moon, also the site of temple ruins. Archeologists visited the lake and its three dozen islands a number of times in the past century or so, to collect stories from the living and to seek the artifacts and the treasures of the dead. Often they found that distinguishing ancient from modern construction was frustrating, for the local people were accustomed to taking stones from the walls, for example, to use in new houses or walls.

The military government was attempting reforms that would improve social and economic conditions for the indigenous people, including the Quechua or Runa, and the Aymara. But removing the private landowners in favor of cooperative agriculture had not automatically brightened the lives of villagers high in the Altiplano.

In 1973-74 the islands of the lake were still considered remote. Since the area offered little in the way of tourist facilities, it was not yet heavily visited by ordinary tourists, although hydrofoils did already crisscross the lake. If income from visitors was minimal, the impact was minimal as well: the native ways of life were not yet preserved in museums.

On a rainy January day the travelers drove from the square to a jetty on the shore of Lake Titicaca. Jones started to run, but slowed to a walk because of the thin air. He walked waist-deep into the lake.

"Then I bent and cupped my hands, drinking in the clear, fresh water, giving thanks to God for letting me survive all the dangers and perils of the last few years long enough to live this moment. As I straightened up, the thunderheads in the distance faded and a bright rainbow, sharper and more vivid than any I had ever seen before, arched across the Lake, bridging the sky from the peak of Sorata to the gleaming silver heights of Illampu, way over in the south, more than one hundred miles away. Bands of brilliant color curved across the heavens, framing the Island of the Sun."

He stood in the icy water, oblivious to everything else. And then, "Sunbeams streamed through the rain clouds in golden shafts, illuminating green, green islands, where before there had been only dark gray, shadowy smudges. As the clouds rolled apart, they revealed the bluest water in the world, and small green parrots flew overhead like emeralds thrown up into the sky."

Soon *Sea Dart* was afloat, her mast raised and rigging set up, flying the burgee of the Royal Naval Sailing Association 12,500 feet above sea level. The engine wouldn't work because of the lack of oxygen and the watery gasoline, so Jones sculled around to his assigned berth using a long sweep oar, went ashore and said farewell. He and Salomon agreed that *Sea Dart* had beaten the onset of the wet season only by hours.

Warm in *Sea Dart's* cabin that night, Jones listened to the rain on the roof. He had no charts of the lake, Peruvian customs officials would be searching for him, he was nearly broke and he was 300 miles inland. But he had *Sea Dart* and time to write as they sailed the 3,200 square miles of Lake Titicaca.

VI. The Incredible Voyage: Lake Titicaca

Rising early, Jones put the kettle on for tea, released *Sea Dart*'s mooring lines and sculled out onto the Bay of Puno toward totora-reed cover and the floating islands of the Uru (or Uro) Indians.

Suddenly *Sea Dart* stopped, caught in the upper reaches of an underwater grove of *llachon*, trees which grow from the lake bottom almost to the surface. Even *Sea Dart*'s shallow draft was enough to catch in the branches and stop her in the clinging tendrils. Jones hacked at the twining *llachon* and slowly cleared them from her keels.

He next sailed to an Uru island, made of woven totora reed with mainland soil spread on top. This particular group of Uru had lost their boats to the wind. Jones sailed *Sea Dart* over to another floating island nearby, evidently a portion of theirs that had become separated, and caught part of it with a long line. *Sea Dart* and the Uru pulled the second island back to the first, and the people harvested the potatoes from their recovered territory. Jones took two of the men to another settlement where they borrowed reed boats so they could fish again.

During his third night there, a storm blew up and moved the island, *Sea Dart* and the reeds she was anchored into, as much as half a mile.

Jones sailed *Sea Dart* out again onto the lake, where she joined the wind-powered ferries, the small steamboats and the hydrofoils that plied the highest waters on earth, moving people and freight from one town or village to another. And she, her sails bright in the sun, was the only ocean-going vessel among them, sailing among the mountains and the stars — over the brilliant reflections of Illimani and Illampu on the placid waters of the daytime, and among the reflected stars at night. She was sailing toward Isla del Sol, the Island of the Sun, only some 40 miles away, but beyond the Strait of Chucuito in Bolivian waters.

The first major island Jones visited was Taquila, with its thousand-foot high conical mountain, a living Quechua village and ruins from ancient times. Here he met an elder he referred to as Machamachani, a *Quipucamayo* or reader of the knotted strings *(quipu)* which preserve the Quechua history. Machamachani told him tales of Kon-Tiki-Vira-Cocha, the creator, and Manco Capac, the first Inca. A young Bolivian Quechua named Huanapaco, whose father was a leader in the northern faction of their clan, had spent some time in La Paz and spoke Bolivian Spanish. He was able to bridge the gap between the storyteller's Quechua and Jones' Spanish. He also guided Jones on a tour of the stone ruins on the island and of the ancient cemetery where the dead sat in baskets, their knees tucked under their chins.

Jones invited Huanapaco to crew for him, and arranged that the young man would sail with him on the lake and into Bolivia, there to ask his father's permission to continue on to the ocean.

They sailed among the northern islands of the lake for about six weeks, on what Jones called "the most beautiful cruising ground in the world." Huanapaco translated for him when they visited Quechua and Aymara settlements.

Sea Dart sailed in cold rain and hot sun, changeable winds and storms among the small islands. Jones commented that she might be sailing in a zephyr one moment and a hundred-mile-an-hour wind the next. They explored the coast through January under the eye of the condor and gray eagle, and moored by sailing into the reed beds.

In early February, they returned to Taquila to say good-bye, then sailed straight for the Island of the Sun. Though he had lingered on the Peruvian side of the lake for more than a month, Jones professed considerable relief at crossing the invisible line between Peru and Bolivia, removing *Sea Dart* from the reach of Lima's "rubber-stamp caesars" who felt entitled to an import tax of fifty per cent of her value. She would not be completely secure until they officially entered the country at Tiquina.

Officially entered or not, *Sea Dart* was the first ocean-going vessel to reach Bolivia since 1879 — mainly because Bolivia had not possessed a seacoast since losing its coastal province of Antofagasta to Chile in a war over guano poaching. (The controversy over sea access for Bolivia continues today. Bolivia is the only country in South America without a direct connection to the oceans; even landlocked Paraguay has major rivers to carry ship traffic to and from the Atlantic.)

Arriving at the Island of the Sun just before dusk on February 7, Jones dropped *Sea Dart*'s anchor in Kona Bay near Kon-Tiki-Vira-Cocha's own landing point.

Jones reported his meeting with the Aymara *alcalde*, or clan chief, on the island as another minor skirmish. The *alcalde* wanted the sailors to pay to visit the sacred places of his island; Jones refused and threatened to report his conduct to the president of Bolivia. Then, he said, the *alcalde* suddenly became almost abject in his eagerness to escort them to all the points of interest on the island. So he was able to see the sacred stone Titi-cala, the Fountain of the Inca (which is said to be a drainage arrangement for the land above it) and the ancient Inca roads, and return to *Sea Dart* with gifts of food.

For the next several mornings, they worked at charting the island and its surrounding waters. Where he knew of no native or Spanish names for the various points or bays, Jones assigned names of his own choosing as he made his map. The long northwest-to-southeast shore between North Kona Bay and Kona Bay, therefore, begins with *Point Barbara* and ends with *Sea Dart Point*. He noted the locations of ten separate pre-Columbian ruins, Titi-cala (for the temple) and the sacrificial altar, along with two Inca roads and the current villages.

They visited with fishermen and with the smugglers who worked the lake with their square-sailed boats; they climbed nearby islands and marveled at a view that included hundreds of miles of mountains and more than a hundred miles of lake, the distances seeming less because of the clear air. *Sea Dart* waited, anchored below them, with the dippers and storks for company. Back on *Sea Dart* in the evenings, Jones worked on the chart, wrote in his log and prepared magazine articles to send out when they reached a town.

And at night, "The clearest night skies I have ever seen anywhere were over the Lake. Out in the ocean, well clear of the land, perhaps a thousand miles out, the skies are crammed with stars, but on Titicaca there was hardly room for the black sky among the stars! The bright planets and all the major stars were like small moons, their rotundity clearly delineated. The man-made satellites were immediately obvious, like taxicabs on the Epsom Downs course on Derby day. There were literally a million bodies in the sky . . . Many a time I would go topsides and be struck with wonder at the display of the heavens, beautiful beyond words, awe-inspiring in its magnificence."

On February 16, they sailed for the Strait of Tiquina and the Bolivian naval base which overlooked the mile-wide passage between the two halves of Lake Titicaca.

Jones described the smaller half, Huinaymarca, as even bluer than the sapphire Chucuito. Set off by the peaks of Sorata, Illampu and Illimani, each more than 20,000 feet high, and dotted with green islands, this is the freshwater lake, as opposed to the somewhat brackish Chucuito.

Huanapaco went ashore at Tiquina, to make his way to his home village. Jones took *Sea Dart* to the naval base to obtain formal entry papers for himself and the boat. He was promptly seized by the navy, accused of being a communist because of *Sea Dart's* Red Ensign, and jailed. He was awakened on the third night by sounds that turned out to be Huanapaco leading a Bolivian naval officer on horseback through the fresh snow. The commander not only freed him from the cell but welcomed him with a speech and invited him to dinner in the officers' mess. Jones also got a much-needed hot bath, and afterward, a splash of political reality as cold as the waters of the great Lake.

Salvador Allende's elected socialist government in Chile had fallen in September; General Augusto Pinochet had seized power there in a coup supported by the United States. The Bolivian frontier with Chile had been closed for two months, and was not likely to re-open any time soon. The only other way down to the Pacific was through Peru, where Jones and *Sea Dart* were bound to be arrested, fined and most likely jailed for evading customs.

There was no going back.

Trapped, Tristan Jones weighed his options and began searching for a new solution.

He could not return to the Pacific Ocean the way he came up, nor could he go down the way he had planned; therefore, he would have to find a new route back to the ocean, something he had not planned for nor imagined. However, this being Tristan Jones, it would probably be a way no one else had done, would do, or would ever *want* to do.

Jones had already accomplished more than one 'first' on the voyage. Now, he held a hand-written permit to enter Bolivia, the first in nearly a century for a foreign ocean-going vessel. The army, the navy and even the customs service had welcomed *Sea Dart*.

As he left Guaqui, the customs official urged him to stop at the Bolivian Yacht Club in Huatajata. So, after he dropped off Huanapaco at the lakeshore village of Puerto Perez, he followed that suggestion.

He said he found there a most unusual 'yacht club', surrounded by a chain-link fence with barbed wire on top, its perimeter patrolled by armed guards with police dogs. And all the members, he noted, had strong German accents. He learned later that many of these 'Bolivian yachtsmen' were survivors of the battleship *Graf Spee* who roared about the lake on weekends in powerboats, attired almost as if they'd never left the German Navy.

Jones says nothing about the town of Huatajata, which is described in a current tour brochure as "an oasis of modern facilities on the still primitive Bolivian high plateau" and home port for the lake's hydrofoils. Tourists from La Paz stop at the Altiplano and Eco museums there and view a reproduction of Heyerdahl's balsa, *Ra II*; they visit *chullpas* (the mortuary towers, which take their name from the pre-Inca people who built them) and learn about the Uru floating islands, in as little as an hour, before going on to the islands of the sun and moon. The brochure does not mention the Bolivian Yacht Club.

That evening he arrived at Cachilaya creek to meet Huanapaco and a crowd of Quechua, including Huanapaco's father Huanameni, the *alcalde* of the clan, and the *llayca* or medicine man.

Next day, with the arrival of a truckload of beer brought in from La Paz for the occasion, the Quechua performed their clan dances. To the accompaniment of flutes, drums, trumpets, tambourines, bells, cymbals and gong, the festivities began shortly after sunrise with line dances and, as the day and the beer wore on, moved into round dances of courtship and a wild rain dance with the *llayca* taunting the devils; and concluded two hours after sunset, everyone drunk and happy, with an intricate dance to welcome the moon.

Throughout the Bolivian autumn and into the winter (February through June), *Sea Dart* cruised Lake Huinaymarca's deep-blue waters. On the island of Quebraya, Jones said, he and Huanapaco found a pre-Inca necropolis where the people were interred standing, in stone tombs built without mortar, and accompanied by worldly goods such as food, weapons and small bronze figures.

While sailing on the lake, he also studied how the locally built boats were made.

The best-known boats of Lake Titicaca are the balsas made of totora reed, great bundles of the reed being lashed together and formed into unsinkable craft that last for several months before becoming waterlogged. If one of these boats breaks up, its passengers can stay afloat simply by staying put. *Ra II* was built with help from the Aymara of Lake Titicaca.

In addition, the Aymara on the island of Suriqui built lug-sailed cedarwood sloops — the cedar coming from the jungles of eastern Bolivia — constructed on adz-hewn eucalyptus frames. These 50-foot-long craft were and are used to transport goods the length of the lake. The Indians, Jones said, had been sailing them completely dependent on the wind direction; he showed them how to change the rigging so they could sail into the wind.

At last, Jones had worked out a way to get *Sea Dart* back to the ocean. As Sherlock Holmes would have observed, when one eliminates the impossible, what remains, however improbable, must be the solution. In this case, the impossible included both of the existing western routes:

the forward route through Chile, blocked by politics, and the backtrack through Peru, blocked by customs. North and south there was no road, no river. But to the east, he discovered, there were alternatives.

The first step was to haul *Sea Dart* across the inner range of the Andes. Then he could haul her to the Beni and sail down into the Madeira and then to the Amazon; or ship her by truck and train to Buenos Aires; or haul her to Santa Cruz, take her by rail across the Chaco Desert to the Mato Grosso of Brazil, and sail down the River Paraguay to the Plate estuary.

No one he consulted knew much about the Beni and the Madeira except that they were reputed to be wild, hellish portions of the jungle. Shipping *Sea Dart* by rail was far beyond his anticipated means.

That left the three-stage route through the Mato Grosso, also beset with unknowns. It hadn't been done before; there might or might not be a port where the railroad met the river; but he might be able to earn the money for shipping costs in time to make the journey during the spring.

At this point, one could raise the question of why he was so determined to take *Sea Dart* back to the ocean in the first place. With obstacles ranging from politics to piranhas ahead of him, why continue once he had achieved the goal, the grail, of Lake Titicaca? He left or gave up other boats when they had served their purposes. But *why* is not a useful question to ask about an obsession. Besides, Jones did own *Sea Dart*; she was his home. He claimed an attachment to her such as he had apparently not experienced with other boats. They would stay together.

At the end of July, Jones and Huanapaco hiked seven miles out to the main road to hitch a ride into La Paz, where they could check for mail and money. Two days in a row they waited all day for a truck to come by and walked back to the village. On the third day, they got a lift from a truck filled with sailors. By the time they approached La Paz, they had figured out that something was not right. When gunfire started near the airbase, they ducked, rolled and ran from the truck.

It turned out they'd ridden into the middle of an attempted coup by the air force, an attempt broken up when the president, General Hugo Banzer Suarez, parachuted onto the base and personally stopped it.

In the mail, Jones found a letter from Banzer Suarez, asking when he and *Sea Dart* would be passing through La Paz, as he wished to arrange a proper reception for them. At the embassy, cricket gear had arrived from England to supply the Quechua who were learning the game. And at the bank he found that he had accumulated enough money to cover the expenses of the Mato Grosso route. It was time to prepare for the journey east.

VII. The Incredible Voyage: From the Lake to the River

On August 18, with a blizzard raging, Tristan Jones sailed *Sea Dart* to Guaqui, where the customs official insisted the navy's permit would be all the paperwork they needed for the trip.

The truck that would take them to the railroad arrived in the afternoon, and *Sea Dart* was loaded aboard. Jones described Chanko, their driver for the trip east, as a teetotalling *mestizo*, a fellow quite unlike Salomon, but also experienced in handling the high mountain roads. And his truck was a Suzuki that Jones described as modern compared to Salomon's old Ford.

Still, they had traveled only 300 yards from the port when the truck slid off the icy road and into a ditch — there to stay for two days, with *Sea Dart* held firmly in place but at a sharp angle from the horizontal, until a tractor was fetched from La Paz to haul it out.

Once again they enjoyed a festive farewell. And this time, the ice having melted, they inched eastward on roads now made of mud, hoping to cross the rest of the Andes in five or six days and reach the wild, poorly charted Paraguay and Paraná rivers while there was still enough water running for *Sea Dart* to sail to the sea. Jones also wanted to get *Sea Dart* away from the Altiplano's extreme variations in temperature.

The combination of hot days and cold, even snowy nights was beginning to open up her seams.

Their first day on the road was marred by another slide into a ditch, this time at La Puerta del Sol, the main gate of the Tiahuanaco ruins called the 'Cradle of American Man', the capital of a pre-Inca civilization. These people are believed to be the ancestors of the present-day Aymara, and this 50-acre site is one of the most important in the archeological record of the Altiplano. Jones and Huanapaco toured the Tiahuanaco temples while a crew of Indians righted the truck. Then they climbed back aboard to slide and slip downhill to La Paz.

At La Paz, they met with another customs delay. This time, the *aduanero* found the whisper of a 100-peso note convincing enough to let them through, though not without a warning about making sure to have papers next time they wanted to bring a boat past him, and they continued into the city.

The truck broke down in the middle of La Paz, a chassis spring broken. Chanko left to stay with relatives, sending a young nephew to look after the truck. Jones sent Huanapaco to seek out the leaders of *Acción Marítima*, a group dedicated to recovery of the Bolivian seacoast territory, who had sent word they planned to welcome *Sea Dart* to La Paz. He was concerned that the *aduanero* might change his mind and seize the boat.

Chanko was gone four days, returning with money to buy goods he would smuggle back home to sell. He and a mechanic set to work repairing the spring. And then the band arrived.

An army brass band played, naval officers made speeches and President Banzer Suarez presented Jones with a red, yellow and green striped Bolivian maritime ensign — the one and only such ensign, Jones said. The naval officers wrote a note to customs for a permission to pass through to Brazil; but the *aduaneros*, rather than write out a pass, held Huanapaco and decided to seize the boat. Jones and Chanko lit out of downtown as soon as Chanko's nephew brought the news.

Leaving La Paz, they were astounded to find once again Commander de Valdez of the Bolivian Navy come to the rescue, with a truck full of sailors keeping the *aduaneros* under control. And so, at last, they were clear of the capital.

Soon they were past the majesty of Illimani, the 21,000-foot land-mark peak outside La Paz, following the smooth modern version of the Inca silver trail. But they turned east toward Cochabamba on a road built only six years before, already rough and potholed from the snows. Crossing the Cordillera de Andes took two days of crawling along the narrow mountainside trail, the cold becoming more bitter as they climbed higher in the midst of magnificent wild mountains.

At last they were headed downhill, which gave them the right of way on the Bolivian mountain road, and their next 'port' was Cochabamba, the 'City of Eternal Spring', about 1,500 feet lower than the bottom of the bowl where sits La Paz. There, in a city closed for *siesta*, they found Huanapaco waiting for them. He had spent only hours in jail before Commander de Valdez had presented an order for his release, an order signed by the president himself. He had taken a bus to Cochabamba and had fallen asleep while watching for the truck. The bus had passed *Sea Dart* on the narrow road.

The British consul in Cochabamba, an archeologist, gave Jones a Union Jack to drape over the boat and told him to let her know immediately if he had any further trouble with the *aduaneros*.

The next afternoon the crew secured *Sea Dart* for the rough road ahead. When they approached the customs hut, timing their move with the *siesta*, they slipped the truck out of gear to roll silently past the *aduaneros* on the way out of the city.

Crossing the last part of the Andes was the roughest passage yet: the rocky path along the mountainside narrower and steeper, the climb higher. The highest point was Paso Siberia, more than 16,000 feet above sea level, where the road was a rough trail running along the top of a col which Jones described as a narrow shoulder between two peaks — a ledge twelve feet wide at most, with a mile or more drop on either side and clouds blowing hard across the ridge in the freezing cold. Jones and Huanapaco crept along the col, one on either side of the truck, sometimes on hands and feet, to find the path and wave Chanko along.

And then, at long last, they started down. The narrow, winding trail seemed to ease slowly down the mountains, but dropped more than 15,000 vertical feet through the foothills to the lowland city of Santa Cruz, with the Chaco Desert beyond.

The distance from La Paz to Cochabamba is about 250 miles; from Cochabamba to Santa Cruz, another 310 miles. Today, guidebooks warn that even the paved main road from La Paz to Cochabamba is slow going, and the Nuevo Camino (New Road) between Cochabamba and Santa Cruz is recommended for four-wheel-drive vehicles only. Travel conditions seem to have improved only slightly over the past 25 years.

They arrived at Santa Cruz on September 6. Once again they hit a ditch, this time breaking the truck's front axle. There were no cranes or tractors handy, the weekend was beginning, and they had a train to catch on Sunday — a train that ran only once a week across El Chaco, six hundred miles to Corumbá in the Mato Grosso. There a river awaited them, its water level dropping day by day. Missing the train was not an option.

Oxen and horses were still employed in Santa Cruz. The voyagers recruited six horses to haul their truck out of the ditch. Chanko went to town in a farm cart to find a mechanic; Jones bought eight small tree trunks from a farmer and set about stacking them to the height of the truck bed. A mule helped move *Sea Dart* off the truck and onto the free-standing platform. By jacking her up on one trunk and sliding out the trunk above it, they got her down to where she was sitting on her keels on two trunks, ready to roll toward the railroad. With two mules to pull her, *Sea Dart* rolled on the trunks toward the station, through a sandstorm and the hot Chaco sun. Progress was slow but steady, and in 24 hours Jones and Huanapaco and the mules moved *Sea Dart* down five feet from the truck, six kilometers (nearly four miles) to the station, and up four feet to the flatcar.

In the morning, however, they learned that they had loaded her onto a train bound for Argentina.

So they began again, but this time without the mules. Jones and Huanapaco took *Sea Dart* off the flatcar with the jacks and tree trunks, then kedged approximately 500 yards across the railyard to the Brazil-bound train. They dug the anchor into the yard ahead of the boat, then hauled on the sheet winch using a block and tackle, with the tree trunks as rollers once again. By mid-afternoon they were settled again, this time on the right train.

Local people started to join them on the flatcar: Bolivian and Argentine peasants traveling across the desert to bring back provisions they could resell at home, young folk eager to talk about the Beatles (inspired by the 'Liverpool' designation on *Sea Dart*'s stern) and drink beer on the crowded car.

Across the desert they rode, with the train stopping periodically so a crew could get off to straighten the track where the heat had warped it, or repair a broken wooden bridge.

And so they arrived, on September 10, in Puerto Suárez, a border town for which Jones had no kind words at all. He vividly described a collection of shacks, a siding with stinking swamp on either side, and mosquitoes "crowding the night air so thickly that there is hardly room between them to see the giant moths, which smash headlong into every light they can find. Over all this hovers a smothering, dank heat, making for an experience rather like putting your head into an oven full of rotting rats."

The stationmaster in Puerto Suárez insisted that Jones had paid to go to Ladário, and it made no difference that the railroad no longer went to Ladário: he could not stay on the train to Corumbá. He would have to get to Ladário on his own.

Jones had neither the money nor the time to brook any further delay. He knew the waters of the Paraguay were dropping, and he had to reach the river. There was nothing to do but take out the truck jacks again, commandeer some 'sleepers' (creosote-and-grease-soaked timbers from the railyard) and begin kedging, hauling, pushing and clawing toward Ladário and/or the old railroad terminus where a crane and jetty might or might not await them.

The distance to Ladário was sixteen miles. Sixteen miles on the old railbed, the tracks torn out, the way overgrown with brush and vines and infested with snakes. And the river was dropping day by day.

Tristan Jones and Huanapaco moved *Sea Dart* those sixteen miles in twenty-one days, working from before dawn to mid-afternoon, beating the bushes to scare away the snakes, subsisting on short rations of a little rice and a shared can of corned beef per day. Fried grubs supplemented their meager diet until they neared the river and were able to catch fish.

Like a mirror image of what he wrote about uneventful and pleasant passages, Jones' account of the inch-by-inch struggle through the scrub is brief. Each day was another brutal haul like the one before and the one to follow, "until it seemed that we had never done anything else but this."

Each day at dawn they began, with cutlass and ax, hacking a passage through the brush eight feet wide, just wide enough to move *Sea Dart* forward, and a hundred yards at a time. They used the kedge or tied a mooring line to a bush and then winched forward, simultaneously beating the grass and bushes to keep snakes at bay. On the two-mile uphill stretch, though it was only a slight grade, they moved inch by inch. The downhill required an additional block to keep *Sea Dart* from sliding down. They worked in suffocating heat all day, but could not work at night for fear of being attacked by anaconda and jaguars, and of losing the edge of the railbed.

It was a haul to stagger the imagination, a feat of sheer dogged determination that outstrips the legend of Fitzcarraldo, the Irishman who brought a small steamboat across a mountain deep in Peru. For Fitzcarraldo had taken his ship apart, and forced members of a local tribe to haul the pieces from one river to the other.

In Werner Herzog's film version of the Fitzcarraldo story, the title character persuades a tribe to haul a larger steamship over a mountain in one piece. And as in his earlier film *Aguirre: der Zorn Gottes (Aguirre: the Wrath of God)*, 1972, the jungle of Peru became a powerful presence in *Fitzcarraldo* (1982). Both are tales of conquest and mad ambition in the Amazon jungle, nearly surpassed by the ambition of their maker. Creating a legend of his own, Herzog isolated his cast and crew for months in remote corners of South America, where, for the sake of a film, for the fulfillment of one man's vision, they faced the same hazards Jones was confronting.

Herzog saw the jungle as a seething mass of growth and decay, a violent place of predation and death, and Tristan Jones would have heartily concurred. He told interviewers later that it took two years of recovery after this voyage before he could stand to be around house plants!

On September 30, Jones walked ahead to the river and found the jetty rotted through, the ancient steam crane nothing but rust. They would have to hack an angled approach down from the railway embankment to the water, a drop of some forty feet.

They reached the riverbank on October 2. For the next eight days they carved their path out of the bank, *Sea Dart* leaning at a precarious angle above the river. Jones ran a rope around her hull and dug in the anchor to keep her from capsizing.

As they turned the bank into a long slipway, they watched the water level dropping.

At last *Sea Dart* eased into the river. Jones went ahead in the dinghy to drop the anchors, and they slipped *Sea Dart* over the sleepers one more time until she floated, caught by the current but held by the anchors, on the River Paraguay. And despite the wild fluctuations of heat and cold, despite the jolting and pounding she had taken mile after mile from Lake Titicaca, she was still sound. She leaked not one drop.

"*Maravilla!* Marvelous!" was their united response.

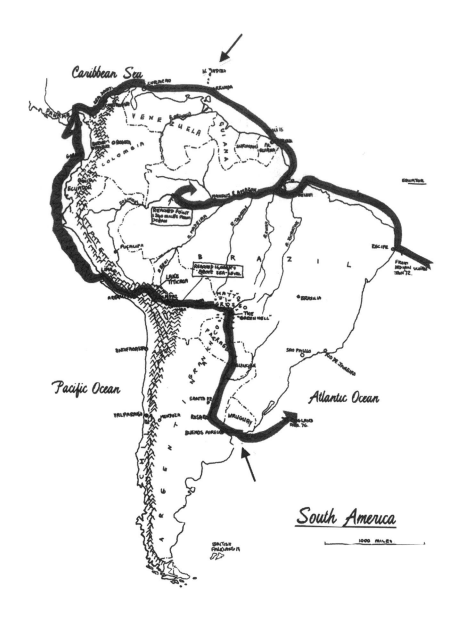

Tristan Jones' voyage with *Sea Dart* began at Bequia (top arrow) and ended off
Uruguay (bottom arrow). FROM *THE INCREDIBLE VOYAGE.*

VIII. The Incredible Voyage: Through the "Green Hell" to the Sea

Sea Dart was afloat once more. Nothing remained between her and the Atlantic but two thousand miles of river. But the first miles consisted of multiple channels meandering through the Mato Grosso, the Great Outback of Brazil.

The word *mato* indicates bush country, wild land with little or no human development. Mato Grosso is the name given to a region of some 300,000 square miles in the center of South America, in the western part of Brazil bordering Bolivia and Paraguay. The name also applies to the state of Mato Grosso, which is part of the region and one of Brazil's larger states; and to a town called Mato Grosso as well, in the western part of the state, north of a great wetland called the Pantanal. South of the Pantanal lies the Mato Grosso do Sul, and this is where *Sea Dart* would drift and sail, along Brazil's western border with Bolivia and Paraguay, until the river carried her back to the open Chaco with its desert and pampas.

The Mato Grosso do Sul is believed to contain even more forms of life than the Amazon Basin. Jaguars, vampire bats, caimans and an astounding variety of birds inhabited the dense and wildly varied forest that included trees such as the *lapacho*, more than 200 feet high and 50 feet around the base.

Reaching the river did not mean clear sailing. The distance from Ladário to Forte Coimbra appears to be about sixty miles in a straight line, roughly a hundred by river. But there are no straight lines in the Mato Grosso.

The map cannot show what those miles are made of. No map can show the shifting multiple channels that thread together to make up the River Paraguay, the trees hanging over the water, the perils that make nighttime movement impossible. Map symbols in the area north and east of the river indicate swamp, and the latitude is a little less than 20 degrees south of the equator. The reality of that tropical swamp is left to the imagination.

In that thick, vine-twined jungle region the many winding, meandering streams often divided into two or three channels, each of which looked as likely as any other. Choosing the wrong channel meant they might drift a mile or more before discovering it was a dead end. Then they climbed overboard into the water, which was sometimes too deep to stand up in, to push and drag *Sea Dart* back against the current. All the while they were beating away caimans, piranha and snakes. Jones also describes lighting a kerosene-soaked rope and passing it over their bodies to burn off the five-inch black leeches that attached themselves while the men were in the water — a scene that brings to mind Humphrey Bogart's torment as he hauled *The African Queen* toward Lake Victoria.

Jones' map depiction of two agonizing days in what he called the 'Green Hell' shows six forays into dead-end channels. On two occasions they drifted well over a mile before discovering their route was not taking them downriver. His map shows the time they reached various points: for example, taking the right fork at 1100 hours, reaching a dead end a mile and a half into the fork at 1300 hours after bashing through a blockage of jungle growth, then fighting their way back for another hour and a half to two hours. Six times in two days, perhaps fifteen daylight hours in total, they drifted into dead ends and had to push *Sea Dart* back to the main channel.

Jones' map shows their entry into that particular stretch of the river at 0700 hours on October 4, and their exit at 2000 hours on October 5, with an overnight stop not quite halfway through. He estimated the direct distance from the start of the maze to its finish at about six miles.

For three weeks they struggled against the jungle, their lives depending on their own hard effort. *Sea Dart* drifted, her sails helping as they could to keep her moving in the right direction. Time and again her crew had to lower the mast to get through the masses of overhanging creepers or trees that leaned across the river. The outboard motor was so much dead weight.

During that three weeks they saw no other human beings, or even any sign of human life. Surrounded by a primeval tangle of impenetrably thick plant life, they drifted and maneuvered among anacondas that dangled from trees to the river to swallow fish whole; among caimans and creeper-laden dead trees.

Exhausted, Jones said he recorded little in *Sea Dart's* log except his estimate of the distance they had moved.

They survived by eating sun-dried piranha, tree leaves and maggoty flour, sharing a can of cold corned beef for Sunday dinner. Their steadily vaporizing kerosene was reserved not for cooking, but for soaking their lines to keep away snakes and ants, and for burning off leeches.

After two weeks, the piranha disappeared from the river and the two men ate everything on board that was even remotely edible: olive oil, linseed oil, wax, a handful of sprouting beans, even the 'stock' they made by boiling a souvenir llama skull. Jones wrote that they agreed that if one of them should die, the other would eat as much of his body as he could stomach.

At a moment of great desperation, they spied a caiman floating in the river. They sailed *Sea Dart* right into the nine-foot reptile, smashed into it with an ax and finished it with a sledgehammer blow. They carved out several pounds of stringy tail meat, went ashore and cooked it, heedless of the ants that overran the area.

After three weeks, the overhanging vegetation gradually thinned out, the streams widened and the current slowed. One night they woke to a sound that Jones compared to an outboard motor roaring. It turned out to be the racket of great moths chewing at the plastic mosquito net that covered *Sea Dart*'s hatch. Beating at the net deterred them, but only dawn ended the attack, which he said left a carpet of moth bodies four inches deep on *Sea Dart*'s topsides.

The next day, *Sea Dart* moved into the swampland and the men sighted smoke some distance away. The humid jungle would not catch fire, nor would the wet swamps: therefore, smoke meant human activity. Never mind that the humans in that area were the Guaycuruan tribes, who were noted for their aggressiveness. In this impossible place, any fellow member of the human species was a link with a world where something existed besides the crawling, seething, roiling 'Green Hell' they had just come through.

They might welcome the sight of fellow humans, but they kept an assortment of weapons close at hand. Any attacker would meet with a harpoon, a distress flare, a sledgehammer *and* a cutlass!

In the event, their first sighting of a human since Puerto Suárez, after a total of five weeks, was as uneventful as it was surprising. They sailed around a bend in the river and saw a man standing in a dugout canoe, fishing with a spear. The fisherman, his naked body smeared with a red mixture of blood, dung and earth, was startled into immobility as they passed. The pair in the boat had no time to assemble their defenses before they were downstream and out of his reach. They kept careful watch the rest of the way to the main River Paraguay.

And on October 25, they came to Paso de Moros, where a rock shelf created rapids roughly 200 yards long, the last obstacle before the main river.

Jones spied a gap near one bank and aimed *Sea Dart* for it, hoping she had enough speed to reach the less turbulent part of the tumultuous passage. Eddies clutched at her, spray flew in all directions, and they could only hope the rudder would keep her headed into the current. Turning broadside would end her journey in less time than it would take to tell the story.

"In the 200 yards or so of rapids we *hit the bottom* with the three keels at least twenty times. We didn't float, we were *pushed* over the flat stone bottom, sliding on the keels with a terrible jarring shudder . . . The last three bumps were the worst — Slam! Bang! Crash! The whole boat shivered and shuddered: the hull, the mast, the keels, the deck —

if anyone had told me that a boat of her size and construction could withstand this encounter, I would not have believed it. But *Sea Dart* did!"

They were through the rapids. *Sea Dart* passed from the slow, winding jungle river through frothing whitewater to deeper and calmer waters in mere moments. And just before nightfall they arrived, ragged and haggard, *Sea Dart* filthy, at the 200-year-old Brazilian army outpost, Forte Coimbra.

Brazilian soldiers helped the sailors ashore for baths, disinfecting and sedative-assisted rest, and also cleaned up *Sea Dart*. The *comandante* and his contingent were the first to hear Jones' story of the or deal in the Mato Grosso. The voyagers stayed some five days, three of them in sick bay, then were ready to move along.

Jones also mentions stopping at Puerto General Busch, the last Bolivian outpost on the River Paraguay, where a monument marks the place where Bolivia, Brazil and Paraguay meet.

"It is probably the only place on earth where you can sail between three countries without challenge, without paper inspections or tax impositions, or any of the rest of the legalized extortion that has crept into international travel," he observed.

Within a day of passing the monument, they arrived at Bahía Negra, Paraguay, which was still too remote for customs or tax authorities to care much about papers and permissions. Their first impression of Paraguay was of music, handsome people and a shortage of men — the last, the result of wars in the nineteenth century and in the 1930s that devastated two separate generations of Paraguay's male population. Some 80 per cent of the men of Paraguay died in the War of the Triple Alliance (1865-1870) against Brazil, Uruguay and Argentina.

More than a century later, in 1995, Paraguay joined with these same three countries in the Mercosur Common Market.

The Chaco War (1929-1935), a dispute with Bolivia over the 97,500-square-mile Chaco plains west of the River Paraguay, also helped bring General Alfredo Stroessner into power. Stroessner's dictatorial regime ruled Paraguay from 1954 until 1989, when he was brought down in a coup. He and his secret police were firmly in charge when *Sea Dart* sailed down the river. Welcoming and pleasant as the

Paraguayan people might be, they lived in a nation whose history was thick with repression and political persecution.

Day by day, village by village, *Sea Dart* and her crew made their way down the river, traveling at about four knots of current and sometimes as much as an additional two knots with sail. The river was wide and clear and contained few dangers. They visited with people in the towns and in settlements too small to be called towns, shared their venison and caught fish for themselves. While still feeling the effects of the heat, they regained much of the weight they had lost in the Mato Grosso.

The sun is at its strongest in Paraguay during the summer months from October to February; locals observe a three-hour *siesta*, preferably indoors. But Jones makes no mention of *siesta*, only of tending the tiller nonstop to contend with the current and eddies while Huanapaco kept the sails trimmed tight to catch some tiny breeze or a turn of the wind that might in a moment send them on a broad reach or running free downriver.

At the mouth of the River Apa and a nearly abandoned San Lazaro, they left Brazil behind. As they sailed the twists and turns of the river, with Paraguay now stretching on either side, they observed the changing land: jungle gave way to desert, desert to scrub, and then scrub yielded to the grassy expanse of the pampas. To the east the panorama was one of transition and change; to the west was the drier, more open Chaco, the territory that had been disputed for so many years at such a high cost to the people of the surrounding nations.

Along the river they encountered bands of *gauchos*, the cowboys of the pampas, who shared their campfires and freshly killed beef, along with wine and stories, well into the moonlit nights.

And so they made their way to Concepción, which Jones compared to the American frontier towns of the 1850s: a single main street, a bank with armed guards, a policeman or soldier on each corner, saloons with hitching posts out front for the horses. Electric power was sketchy, and grass grew in the streets. Though they found the people friendly, the travelers were too depleted, physically and financially, to linger. They pushed on to Asunción.

Along the way they encountered a British merchant ship — it was registered in Liverpool, just as Jones claimed he had registered *Sea Dart* — at work a thousand miles upriver from the Atlantic. And they sighted an Argentine river vessel as well, evidence that they were approaching the last country between them and the ocean.

Arriving in Asunción on November 18, they first had to run the gamut of officialdom, taking care of the paperwork for "entering the country" after having sailed 700 miles through it. This entailed the kind of routine that, country after country, evoked some of Jones' most passionate outbursts of protest in his written accounts. Then they visited the British embassy, hoping for a stack of mail and money, and found only a bill from the income tax authorities in England.

Jones and Huanapaco spent the next several days meeting the people of the capital, from a storytelling pie-seller to President Alfredo Stroessner himself. As Jones tells it, Stroessner arrived one afternoon with an eight-officer bodyguard, demanding to come aboard. Hearing Huanapaco telling a visitor he would have to wait for the captain's permission, Jones popped up to the deck and allowed Stroessner aboard, but without his guard. He asserted that *Sea Dart* was British territory, and British law did not allow armed men aboard unless the captain requested them; besides, their weight would sink the boat. Stroessner agreed, and came aboard to talk about small craft. Jones told stories of his voyages, and Stroessner promised to keep the customs authorities from harassing him.

Once the mail arrived, including some money, the sailors indulged in fresh food, ice cream, cold beer and other pleasures. They left Asunción feeling refreshed and ready for the 400-mile journey to the mouth of the river. Early in December they passed the ruins of Humaita, once called the 'Gibraltar of the Jungles' and an important site in the War of the Triple Alliance; a few miles further, the current pulled them into the wild Paraná, the broad river that would take them to the sea.

In the city of Paraná, only a few miles from the mouth of the Paraguay, they entered Argentina with the proper papers, carefully secured at the Argentine embassy in Asunción. They were welcomed as explorers and heroes, and interviewed by the local newspaper. But that evening, they were stopped by security police, taken to the police station and detained in a crowded holding cell.

This was the routine greeting for strangers in town: detention, a check of the central records agency, and then, provided the person had a clean record, release in one (or several) days. People with criminal records were detained in the local jail for weeks; many *politicos* disappeared completely. Jones and Huanapaco were singled out the next morning and released, officials exclaiming, "Why didn't you tell us who you were? This is all totally unnecessary! Enjoy your visit!"

They enjoyed their visit all the way back to the mooring barge, where *Sea Dart* was tied up waiting for them. They headed across the river to Santa Fe posthaste, where they added *Sea Dart's* name to those on the wall of the jetty. At the Santa Fe yacht club, they were welcomed and honored; and after two days, *Sea Dart* headed south again.

Soon afterward, *Sea Dart* encountered the *pampero* for the first time. A powerful wind out of the west to southwest, the *pampero* sweeps up from the extreme southern region of Patagonia across the pampas. On the Paraná, two thousand miles from its beginnings, the *pampero* was heavy with dust and still strong enough to pile up waves, turn the river into whitewater, even force the flow of the river backward. Jones said the temperature dropped seventy degrees in four minutes, the wind producing frost on the pampas grasses on what had been a hundred-degree summer day.

Seeing the distinctive low, cigar-shaped cloud that heralded the *pampero,* Jones and Huanapaco secured *Sea Dart* with two anchors set into the riverbed and six mooring lines on heavy, 10-foot stakes of the uniquely hard wood called *palo blanco,* leaving only a foot of each stake above ground. The sailors watched the water rush back upstream as the sky filled with dust. The anchors and stakes held against the wind.

They continued downriver, calling at various ports along the way, aiming to arrive at San Nicolás before Christmas. Boat handling required full attention to both sails and tiller in the wild channels and currents of the great Paraná, which sometimes ran as much as thirty miles wide.

At San Nicolás, Jones wrote, he had gifts from the Holy Land to present to the yacht club, but the club would not allow Huanapaco to attend their dinner. Once again the sailors stuck together, heading back to *Sea Dart* and the dark river.

Coming into the delta of the Paraná, they found the land changed again from scrub to swamp and jungle. The river became another watery maze of channels that continued for 200 miles to the estuary, the Rio de la Plata. There the waters of the Paraná meet the Paraguay, the Bermejo and the Uruguay, and rush into the Atlantic. *Sea Dart* sailed briskly into the maze, her handlers keeping her in the deep water and avoiding hazards that included islands, sunken trees and wrecked boats.

They reached San Isidro, a fishing port, on December 23, and then pushed on into a branch of the river delta called El Tigre. Before noon on Christmas Eve, they were in the Rio de la Plata, which opens out to 140 miles wide, with clear sailing to Buenos Aires and the Yacht Club Argentino. Jones describes their arrival:

"In the center of one of the busiest seaports in the world, with ocean steamers moored by the dozen, tiny *Sea Dart* crept in on the weakening evening breeze, her grubby, patched sails only just edging her forward, her worn hull blistered by the hot sun of the pampas, her mast scarred and scratched by the cruel overhanging jungle thorns of the Mato Grosso, and anchored at the guest-of-honor mooring. She crept in like a wayward child and quietly settled down only yards from the haughty clock-tower which sticks up like an admonishing finger in the center of the Buenos Aires docks . . . We'd done it! For the first time ever in recorded history a sea-going boat had crossed right through the middle of South America! We had sailed *Sea Dart* thousands of miles where no sail had ever been before!

"I had taken the ocean to Bolivia and had brought Bolivia back down to the ocean! I had seized for Britain the altitude sailing record of the world, unbeatable until man finds water on a star! I had reached three *impossible* destinations — the Dead Sea, Lake Titicaca, and then the Atlantic through the living death of the Mato Grosso! Slowly, little by little, as *Sea Dart* progressed down the populated areas of the Argentine, she had become a living legend."

She had also taken a beating such as few boats her size could survive. She had been shaken and jarred from mast to keels; and the alternating heat and cold had opened her seams. Tough though she was, she was in no condition to sail any further.

IX. After the Voyage

Looking back at the Christmas Eve he had spent in Bethlehem nearing the first of his "three impossible destinations" with *Barbara*, Jones said he celebrated the Christmas of 1974 and the completion of the incredible voyage in company with Huanapaco, dining on corned beef and drinking cold beer. They acquired their repast on credit, since a nearby bar was open and the banks and embassies were closed, and observed their holiday on the waterfront.

Their next order of business after Christmas was to collect the money waiting for Jones in Buenos Aires and apply it to get themselves into shape again. Both were treated for parasites and general tropical deterioration. Jones said doctors removed a four-foot tapeworm that had been keeping him hungry for weeks. Each man had lost considerable weight, and they set out to remedy that situation as quickly as possible.

In late January, Huanapaco returned to the heights of Bolivia, traveling this time by plane. Several weeks later, in March, after a rough time at the hands of the Argentine police, Jones hauled anchor and "limped west along the coast to the small fishing port of Olivos, about eight miles along the shore." He struck the Red Ensign, painted *Sea Dart*'s topsides gray and concealed her name, trying to make her blend in among the local vessels. There he continued his recovery, wrote his articles and began to prepare *Sea Dart* for her next voyage. He planned to sail across the Plate estuary to Montevideo, Uruguay, about 140 miles in a straight line.

Between January and July, Jones said, he was picked up three times and held by the police for two days and two nights at a time, released on each occasion with no charges. At that time, the police were routinely taking people into custody without any charge, just as they had in Paraná. Jones wrote of the vicious brutality by the jailers and policemen, brutality that went unchecked and unreported in the police state that was Argentina in the 1970s.

But price subsidies made it an inexpensive country for a low budget traveler such as Jones. He wrote of buying dinner and seeing a show any night he chose, and returning to the boat with change left from five dollars. Between arrests he worked on the boat or wrote articles for sailing periodicals around the world.

By mid-May, he figured *Sea Dart* was ready for the passage to Montevideo. According to his account in *The Incredible Voyage*, he then started on the seemingly interminable round of paperwork and officialdom that he had to run to gain permission to leave the country. In mid-July, however, he had enough money from articles to stock the boat. He wrote that he feared the consequences of applying for an exit permit — feared that he and/or *Sea Dart* would be arrested on political grounds — so he quit fighting Argentina's bureaucracy and simply sailed out of Olivos at two a.m. on July 14, under cloudy skies.

Steering *Sea Dart* carefully through the buoyed channels, he was close to the Uruguayan shore by morning. He continued to sail through the next night. On the second morning, a mile or more off the sandy beaches and green hills of the Uruguayan shore with their craggy rock outcroppings, Jones was enjoying his cross-continental triumph and thinking about the next leg of the voyage. He had decided to head for Rio Grande do Sul, a 600-mile passage north to the southernmost state in Brazil.

About eight miles out of Montevideo, the chilly northeasterly wind turned to something much more dangerous. The rocky shore was too close for comfort, but the narrow channels of the Rio de la Plata prevented *Sea Dart* from sailing out away from the shore.

The *cigarro*, the black wind cloud that signaled the approach of the *pampero*, appeared suddenly in the early afternoon. Realizing there was only about a mile of water, mud and sand between *Sea Dart* and the shore, Jones pulled down the genoa, hoisted the number two jib, and headed her out away from shore, toward a great mud bank. The wind rose quickly, turning the shallow estuary into a "seething cauldron" in which *Sea Dart* bounced about "like a landed piranha!"

As the cloud moved closer and the winds rose, the reefed-down mainsail blew out; the jib held, but only on a broad reach. The eight miles to Montevideo might as well have been eight hundred. Ahead of *Sea Dart* was a group of jagged rocks. Her course was straight into them. Neither sail, since he had only the jib, nor the little four-horse-power engine aboard could move her into the wind, or even hold her in place against the *pampero*.

And then the fog fell around her. It was the *cigarro* come down to the sea. Jones set out a 28-pound Danforth anchor and prepared to set the fisherman anchor as well. Before he could send the second anchor overboard, he heard "a crack like doomsday" above him. The Danforth's line, the same inch-and-a-half line that had hauled them out of the ditch at the Tiahuanaco ruins, had broken.

Sea Dart began to drift toward shore with the wind. Helpless against the combined wind and waves, she broached, broadside to the waves, heeling over, slamming sideways. The *pampero*-impelled waters shoved her unmercifully onto solid rock "with a force that shook her small frame to the very keel-bolts."

Jones dragged out the genoa and jammed it under the bilge keel that was buckling against the rock. As the wind backed off slightly and the pounding of boat on stone eased, he started the bilge pump. The damaged stern was rapidly taking on water.

"I never considered the possibility of abandoning her," he recalled. "It would have been impossible to think of that after all we had been through together. I was not going to leave my bloody boat on a f——g South American rock. I had to get her off. She didn't belong here; she was British, and by Christ, back home to Britain she'd go, regardless!" Tempted though he was to give up the fight, he kept on pumping; he pumped water out of the boat, and air into his rubber dinghy, preparing to fight his way off the rock.

He pushed the dinghy over the side, loaded it up with anchor, chain and storm line, and rowed against the violent sea. About 200 feet from *Sea Dart*, he dropped the anchor. Then he rowed back to the boat, pumped water out, secured the anchor line to the jib-sheet winch and began kedging off the rock. He estimated it was two hours, "two hours of hard, heavy heaving, cursing, groaning, and pumping before *Sea Dart* finally started to inch out to the anchor, pounding and bouncing all the while, with me cold, desperate, and wet through."

The wind dropped shortly before the false dawn, and the sea subsided. Jones waited, stowing the damaged mainsail and putting on a storm trysail, pumping water, eating cold corned beef straight from the can, until a northerly wind came up, blowing from the land to fill the small sails. He pulled in the heavy anchor and *Sea Dart* once again headed into the swells, her skipper steering carefully and continuing to pump water from her stern as they moved along the coast.

Before noon on July 17, *Sea Dart* had "tacked her way laboriously right into Montevideo harbor." Jones "ran her hard right up onto a dry mudbank, kicked the anchor over the side, and fell into the deepest sleep I can remember."

After dealing with customs the next morning, Jones calculated his chances of making *Sea Dart* fit to sail again. He could not refit her quickly; if he could obtain the gear he needed, earning the money and refitting her would take a year. Nor, he insisted, could he leave her in South America. He saw only one solution: shipping her home to England.

He arranged to send her to England on the steamship *Hardwicke Grange*, the shipping costs to be paid when he arrived there himself.

"As she sat on deck, looking forlorn but cocky, I walked away, thinking, 'Lionhearted, courageous little bitch. Well, South America tried to get you a thousand times, but in the end, you little bugger, you beat it, you won! You beat a continent!' Through the winter rain of the Montevideo docks, feeling both victorious and bereft, and very, very lonely, I walked on towards the main gate . . .

"Cold and shivering, with icy water seeping through the holes in my only shoes, I turned around to stare over towards the big, brightly floodlit ship. There *she* was, far away through the sabering rain, a small dark hump on the deck. I turned and ran back towards her . . . until at last, breathless, I stood on the departure mole. Under the doleful light of the mole lamps, I waited for the *Hardwicke Grange* to pass. Through the rain, I searched for *Sea Dart*, and as the ship passed majestically by, I saw her . . . She was on her way home, the ragged ensign fluttering on her stern.

"I stared after her, wet through, with wet eyes, until the last glimmer of the ship's lights disappeared. Despondently, I turned towards the sad city and my cheap room.

"A docks policeman stood under the next lamppost, rifle in hand under his streaming cape. His leather chinstrap dripped water, a damp cigarette drooped from his mouth. He waved his free hand lackadaisically as I passed.

'Buenas noches, Señor. You have a friend onboard going to England?'

'Buenas. Yes, she's going to England.'

'She must be very beautiful for you to stand out here in the rain all this time?'

'Si, Señor, the most beautiful in the whole wide world!'

He grinned. 'Some people have all the luck!'"

He had smuggled his gear ashore, including charts, sextant, motor, mooring lines and the rubber dinghy, all of which he sold to a fence. (Ron Reil commented that Jones had told him a sailor should never be separated from his instruments; but by his own account, Jones sold or traded sextants and similar gear several times. The sextant he sold in Montevideo may have been the one that he insisted on getting along with *Sea Dart*. The Center for Wooden Boats, in Seattle, displays an octant whose donor said he received it from Jones in exchange for a movie camera.)

The money from his gear, plus a contribution from a trade unionist and other people he had met in Argentina, paid his airfare back to London.

In the meantime, he was arrested in Montevideo for his association with the union activists, and spent five days in the Liberdad jail. He was released through the efforts of the British embassy and was quick to arrange a flight home. Before July was out, Jones was back in England.

Arriving in London, however, Jones found little to greet him. The friends he had planned to stay with were both dead; he had virtually no money left; and *Sea Dart* was due to arrive shortly at Newhaven, on the southern coast. If he could get to her, he recalled, "I'd be safe." He could live aboard and work and refit her for a new voyage.

So he set off on foot to Newhaven.

There he found that *Hardwicke Grange* had indeed arrived, with *Sea Dart* safely aboard, and his arrangements for freightage were fine. But the customs office required a clearance certificate and payment of the VAT, the Value Added Tax which had come into existence during Jones' seven years out of Britain, because technically, having been sold by Osborne to Reil, she had been "exported." Now, by their reasoning, she was being "re-imported," and there was a matter of 750 pounds sterling due in import tax. The vessel and all its contents — Jones' remaining personal gear — were to be held in bond until the tax was paid.

Again, Jones' contempt for officials, taxes, permits and customs processes flared. He vowed he would "get her out from under this bloody stupid tax," and walked back to London.

He returned to the boiler room at Harrods, where he had studied and figured and planned his quest for the altitude sailing records. He stayed in a Paddington hotel managed by a couple he described only as young Australians, for whom he briefly served as a sailing mentor. They had a catamaran, and sailed it into the English Channel on a short trip that inspired his comment: "I have never been much attracted to catamarans or any kind of multihull vessel . . . I simply do not trust them." Less than ten years later, after the amputation of a leg, he would find the stability of a multihull craft well worth praising, and would take a trimaran called *Outward Leg* across Europe and eastward.

This stint at Harrods, during which Jones started writing the first draft of *The Incredible Voyage*, lasted only a month, but helped him to get back on his feet again. When an American delivery skipper called with an offer of a 50-foot boat to sail from Long Island to the West Indies, Jones was ready to go. The trip would give him time to write and money toward *Sea Dart*'s freedom. Told that he had to find a cook for the voyage, he replied with typical Jonesian understatement, "I'll drag a cook out of hell if it will get *Sea Dart* out of hock."

From that sailing job to the next, working as a dinner-cruise skipper in New York, and wherever he went, Jones carried his portable typewriter and his manuscripts, continuing to pour the stories of *Barbara* and *Sea Dart* onto page after page. He told his tales to everyone he met. When he wasn't living on a boat, he stayed in New York's cheapest hotels and a men's shelter; and wherever he worked, he sent a piece of his pay to England, to pay *Sea Dart*'s shipping and mooring costs.

He wrote *The Incredible Voyage,* he said, because it had to be written. It was, in part, an exercise in self-discipline; but it also sprang from his fear of losing *Sea Dart* and being stranded. He wrote constantly, twelve hours a day, every day, for nine months, he said in *Adrift.* To write the whole story "would be impossible to do in less than a million words," but he cut it down to 120,000 words written in three rapid drafts and completed it in late October 1976. He took the manuscript to a New York publisher and was told it would be considered in about a month.

Meanwhile, *Sea Dart* waited in a shed, dockside, in England, for the settling of accounts and her freedom.

As Jones tells it, the breakthrough in their circumstances came about by what some might consider coincidence. One of the men who had crewed for him on the first trip from New York to the West Indies called with an improbable story: a man, with the same name as his, had seen ads for his business and had stopped to meet him. In their conversation, the crewman had told him about his trip with Jones. The visitor, who was a shareholder in a publishing company, thought the company might be excited about *The Incredible Voyage.* Jones retrieved his manuscript, as yet unread, from the New York publisher and submitted it to the publishing house in Kansas City, which was immediately interested.

In early December, Jones met with the publisher, whose first question was, "How's the boat?" Jones told him she was still impounded for tax and he was determined not to pay, even though a member of Parliament had gotten the customs authorities to reduce the amount of import tax due by half. (Jones had gone so far as to write to Prince Philip seeking relief.)

"If I had another advance . . . " he said, and the publisher agreed. They worked out a three-book contract, with an advance sufficient to pay the balance of *Sea Dart's* passage to England, her storage in Newhaven, insurance and her passage to the United States — without a penny for import tax to British Customs. *Sea Dart* and Jones then would embark on a cross-country tour to promote the book, *The Incredible Voyage.*

"All I could sense," he wrote later, "was the trembling of little *Sea Dart's* hull on the windswept jetty of Newhaven, four and a half thousand miles away . . . A wooden ship lives . . . I owed her a debt beyond money for her past loyalty to me." And so Jones arranged for *Sea Dart* to be shipped to the United States in April, and lined up a free berth for her.

In the meantime, he visited the Explorers Club, where a member told him they were planning their annual dinner in mid-April, with fifteen hundred prominent people in attendance. He was invited to speak — it was a perfect opportunity to talk about the need for people to care for the ocean — and wouldn't it be something, they agreed, if *Sea Dart* accompanied him. She was due to arrive several days before the event, which would take place in the fourth-floor ballroom of the Waldorf-Astoria Hotel.

"And where else should I take a little heroine arriving in New York," he asked, "but to dinner in one of the best hotels?"

As usual, once Tristan Jones set his mind to a project, nothing could stand in the way of its accomplishment.

He scouted the hotel. The passage would be tight at best. Then he waited. Delays brought *Sea Dart's* arrival date uncomfortably close to the date of the dinner; but at last she was due to arrive in Bayonne, New Jersey, on April 14. The dinner was the next evening.

Both anxious and eager, Jones arrived early at the docks to discover that the longshoremen who would normally unload the cargo were threatening to strike. But he found a sympathetic listener and the promise of help.

His companion watched in admiration as several yachts, some of them fifty feet or more, came off the ship. Then he saw tiny, bedraggled *Sea Dart* waiting her turn to disembark.

"You go to sea in *that?*" he asked in amazement.

Jones confessed to a welling of emotion and a need to spend a few private moments with *Sea Dart* before the longshoremen unofficially brought her off the ship, onto a truck, and on her way to the heart of New York City.

Bringing the boat into the city was easy; getting her into the Waldorf-Astoria and up to the ballroom was another matter entirely. Riding on a low trolley, she slipped through the kitchen with hardly a gap on either side, and then came to the hotel's freight elevator. Small as she was in the world of boats, *Sea Dart* was too long. Jones sacrificed her cobbled-together bowsprit, sawing it off himself in his determination. By setting her spritless and angled into the elevator on the diagonal, he took her up to the fourth floor. There they encountered the doorway, not quite high enough even with the trolley tires deflated. Someone suggested she be displayed in the hall; but that would never do. Out came the saw again, and her doghouse roof was gone, making just enough of a difference to slip her into the ballroom at last. Jones set the sawn pieces back in place and draped her with flags.

That evening, after their traditional dinner of exotic dishes from around the world, the Explorers Club members heard five speakers. The last of them was Tristan Jones, talking about his voyages and the plight of the oceans.

But the star of the evening was a battered, sawn-off little cutter that stood silently, solidly on her three keels, draped with flags and bearing the scars of her implausible voyage from the West Indies to Montevideo. Celebrities came up to her platform after the program, signed their names on her hull, and paused to contemplate all that she represented. There, among the other world adventurers, she was truly among friends.

The guests, in their evening clothes, helped move *Sea Dart* back out of the ballroom and down to the street. And Jones slept aboard that night, another destination reached, another unique voyage completed.

Their next voyage, the national tour to promote *The Incredible Voyage*, began the next morning with a mule team — recalling the mules of Bo-

Tristan Jones and *Sea Dart* in the ballroom of the Waldorf-Astoria Hotel. SHERIDAN HOUSE ARCHIVES.

Sea Dart after her tour of the United States. Autographs are visible on her bow, and the patched scar of her South American ordeal on her stern. PHOTO BY TRISTAN JONES.

livia — to haul *Sea Dart* through the streets of Manhattan for three days, touring everything from Times Square to Central Park. Children clambered all over her wherever she stopped. Driving by the park, he was tempted to launch *Sea Dart* on the pond, or put her on rollers and sail her right down Fifth Avenue.

In June, *Sea Dart* was loaded onto a flatbed truck for her tour of the United States. Their first stop was the Explorers Club, where newsman and sailor Walter Cronkite came aboard. Then they drove to the Bowery, where Jones stopped to greet men he had met while living one step from the streets.

Continuing around the country, Tristan Jones and *Sea Dart* visited Washington, D.C.; Pittsburgh, Pennsylvania; St. Louis, Missouri; and dozens of other cities. "[*Sea Dart*] was to be hauled right across the United States from Boston to Seattle. She would touch the Canadian border in the north, she would, it was intended, sail down the Mississippi from Minneapolis to St. Louis and she would touch the Mexican border in the south." In each 'port of call' people came to see the boat and hear her story.

Tom Thornton was Director of Sales and Marketing for the publisher Andrews & McMeel at the time of the *Sea Dart* tour. Now president of Andrews McMeel Universal, he describes the tour as "not without incident." In fact, he said, it was a "logistical nightmare," hauling the strapped-down boat on a leased flatbed truck in the hot summer. The truck's driver for the first part of the trip was a 19-year-old Universal Press Syndicate mailroom employee who quit the company after driving to New York and touring through Pittsburgh, Washington and other cities with Tristan Jones in the passenger seat.

Thornton vividly recalls his years working with Jones, including the two a.m. calls he received from the author, whose hot temper flared when not enough people showed up for a signing, or arrangements were not to his liking.

A second driver completed the western half of the tour, but called Thornton from Seattle, in front of the Seattle *Post-Intelligencer* building, to say he wanted a plane ticket home. Thornton pointed out to him that he did have to drive the truck back to Kansas City, and asked, "What's Tristan doing?"

"He's wiping his face," the driver said. "I hit him."

Regardless of his troubles on the tour, Jones did draw adventure lovers, sailors and children to his signings, and would stand and talk to someone for half an hour at a time.

"He loved to talk and he loved the boat," Thornton said.

And the boat caused them no trouble at all. Strapped down to the flatbed, she toured the nation "like the gentle lady that it was supposed to be," Thornton said. "And Tristan lived up to his legend" as they traveled west through Denver, southwest to Texas and Arizona, then through California to Portland and, ultimately, Seattle.

In Oregon, Ron Reil caught a brief story on the television news about *Sea Dart*'s appearance in Portland.

"That's my boat!" he told his wife in amazement.

X. On Puget Sound

Tristan Jones and *Sea Dart* ended their book tour in Seattle, Washington. Jones placed *Sea Dart* in care of a boat storage yard on the waterfront of Edmonds, just north of Seattle, and returned to New York and his typewriter. He had three more books to write.

And there she sat on her sturdy keels, forklifted into a corner of the yard. Jones, or rather his publicist, paid the storage charges month by month, and *Sea Dart* waited.

One day in 1979, a young boatwright named Mark Rice set out for a walk along the railroad track which runs through the Edmonds waterfront area. Familiar with the *Sea Dart* story from Jones' appearance on the television program "To Tell the Truth," as well as from reading *The Incredible Voyage*, Rice recognized *Sea Dart* at once.

He was 22 years old, working as a mechanic for Alaska Marine Engines in Seattle and dating the daughter of a federal judge. Powerboats were, and for many years would remain, his specialty. He was, at first glance, an unlikely champion for a sailboat. But Mark Rice had loved boats of all kinds "since I was knee-high to a duck." He had served in the army and worked on a fishing boat, and then gotten caught up in the marine industry.

"Once you've been on a boat, it's hard to step off 'em," he said twenty years later.

Though his sailing experience was limited, his interest in *Sea Dart* was enthusiastic. Rice obtained the address of Jones' publicist from the storage yard owner, and wrote to express his concern about the condition of the boat and her being stored out in the open.

He wanted to restore and preserve her: his interest was historical more than practical. He felt that whether *Sea Dart* ever sailed again or not, "she needed to be kept."

Rice sought the advice of his girlfriend's father, the judge. And he enlisted the assistance of the judge's clerk, David Feigelson, and another young lawyer, David Yetevsky. Yetevsky drew up the articles of incorporation for Sailing Craft Restoration and Preservation (SCRAP) in one lively evening at the Blue Moon Tavern, a popular watering hole near the University of Washington.

In December, Rice and Feigelson received a letter from Jones:

Dear Messrs Feigelson and Rice,
    Your letter has reached me like a trumpet blast from the U.S. cavalry. Briefly, I am both bound and gagged by my writing commitments — and torn between abandoning them and heading to *Sea Dart,* or abandoning *Sea Dart.*
    It may be hard for you to understand, but I have been trying to shove the spirit of sail into places and heads where it has never been . . . I have been in touch with the Sea Cadet Association of New Jersey . . . I offered them *Sea Dart* — I even offered to pay for her transport back to New Jersey — but they seem to have lost interest . . . .
    Therefore *Sea Dart* is still my own property, clear of encumbrance and if you agree to the following I will transfer her ownership to you:
    (1) *Sea Dart* will not be re-sold by you for profit.
    (2) If you wish to divest yourself of ownership of *Sea Dart* you will donate the craft to an organization (non-profit) concerned with the education and training of young people.
    If you agree to this I will send you a formal letter, together with a check for $500.00 toward her restoration, and her documents.

Note: the reason for the above conditions is that *Sea Dart* is a British vessel, and was allowed into the United States in perpetuity on condition that she was not used for gain. I am certain there would be no flak from the Customs whatever happens, but I wish to keep my private word to the U.S. Customs.

If I can help in any other way, restricted as I am for the next year or so, I will be happy to do so . . . .

In a follow-up letter the next day, Jones told the SCRAP organizers he had learned that it would be more to his advantage for tax purposes to sell *Sea Dart* to them as a salvage sale after the first of the year, and send them the donation in April.

"In this way," he wrote, "I can claim a tax allowance against depreciation of the vessel since 1977. It is better than an outright donation of the boat to you, because it saves a whole mess of paperwork with IRS and Customs."

He noted in the same letter that he had "several mementoes of the South American calvary, including the painted flag worn on Lake Titicaca and the first Bolivian maritime flag ever made, in a rather tatty state, but nevertheless . . . it was presented to me by President Banzer (whom Allah preserve!) when I shot and was shot at, through La Paz."

And he promised that "when you have the boat in display order, [I shall] send you her logbook of the Voyage."

Meanwhile, Rice had moved to Friday Harbor on San Juan Island. In January 1980, he received the ownership papers and logbook. He wrote to Jones about his plans for publicity and a meeting with the Children's Home Society, and stated, "Our love for this boat is great and our determination to restore the *Sea Dart* knows no bounds."

Once the transfer of ownership was complete, he brought *Sea Dart* home to the island to begin what he hoped would be a community restoration effort. He was living in one of the most sailing-oriented parts of the Pacific Northwest, on an island that was home to hundreds, perhaps thousands of sailing craft. Surely *Sea Dart* would find many friends there.

He began by cleaning the boat.

"There was a foot of water in the bilge!" he recalls. Stored outside as she was, *Sea Dart* had not received much protection from Seattle's rains and generally damp weather. There were indications of vandalism as well from a break-in at the storage facility in Edmonds. But mostly what Rice found was a sludge of 'historic' refuse, soaked and rotten, in the bottom of the boat.

"I found *piranha skeletons* in that bilge!" he says. "Skeletons and bones — and the stink was unbelievable." Clearly, he said, "housekeeping was not a part of [Jones'] life," and two years in storage had only made matters worse.

It was clear to Rice that Jones, for all his protestations, had simply walked away from *Sea Dart* leaving everything aboard, from a wall plaque with a prayer attributed to Joshua Slocum, to underwear floating in the bilge.

Since so much of what was left in and on the boat was beyond use or repair, "so wasted you couldn't resurrect it," in Rice's words, he didn't try to salvage all of it. Instead, over the next several years, some of the smaller bits of the gear he could salvage were given or traded away, often as prizes for youngsters in island races or regattas. The trail (taffrail) log, for one, went to a young rowing-contest winner who, Rice said, never really believed her prize came from *Sea Dart*.

Rice traded the fisherman anchor that had held *Sea Dart* in the *pampero* to Dick Barnes, owner of a local resort, who provided him with a place to work on the boat.

"Tristan Jones borrowed and traded to make it happen," Rice points out.

Beyond the cleanout, months of work lay ahead to put *Sea Dart* back on the water.

Nordine Jensen, of Albert Jensen and Sons Shipyard in Friday Harbor, performed a survey of *Sea Dart* and told Rice the boat had "no monetary value" in its current condition. He estimated it would cost about $3,000 in materials alone, not to mention labor, to render her seaworthy.

So Rice cleaned out the bilges, sorting through the debris Jones had left behind, and finally working on the boat itself. He worked on *Sea Dart* at Snug Harbor Resort, at Jensen's boatyard while he was employed there, and later at his own place in the middle of San Juan Island.

Over the next two years, he removed a dozen or more coats of tar from the bottom (Ron Reil notes those layers "may be the 21 coats of Limpitite hull coating that Osborne was so proud of. It is a black rubber-like substance that I had to deal with in some of my hull work too."). He scraped the painted hull with its autographs — those of Walter Cronkite and "two or three Miss Americas" among them. He scraped, sanded, painted and repaired what he could, assisted from time to time by classes of high-school students. These, he said, were the hard-to-handle kids for whom the boatwork was part of the school's attempt to cope with their behavior.

He tried to re-do the mast, but it was eaten by saltwater and be-yond repair. He had the metal bilge keels removed and re-galvanized. A boatbuilder on Orcas Island nearby planned to build some blocks for the boat; Rice left the keels with him.

Rice probably knows *Sea Dart*, at least *Sea Dart* after South Amer-ica, as intimately as anyone. As a boatbuilder, he commented that she "wasn't real well built in the first place," certainly not built to present-day standards.

Rice put all the money he could into the boat, and she was nowhere near ready to sail. He recalls that comments were published in a boat-ing magazine taking him to task for not working on the boat, reporting that it was upside down in a field and suffering neglect.

"It was upside down," Rice says, "because we were working on it." He said he suffered bad press because well-to-do 'boat snobs' wanted *Sea Dart* for themselves, and they couldn't have her. They weren't help-ing him with the restoration, either. In fact, according to some accounts, people were helping themselves to bits and pieces of the boat as sou-venirs. But Rice had given his word to Tristan Jones, a man he regarded as a hero, and he was not about to break it.

Early on, while Rice had custody of *Sea Dart*, Tristan Jones came to San Juan Island for a visit that included two days of sea stories and con-siderable drinking. Jones also went to Victoria to see the historic boats in a museum there. Dick Barnes, familiar with *Sea Dart*'s adventures, re-called Jones from that visit as "lean and focused as a person," someone who would take on tasks that "the rest of us mere mortals" would never try.

Rice met with Jones once again at the Pacific Science Center in Seattle, to receive the *Sea Dart* logbook, which included stamps from the places Jones had taken her, along with slides which Rice gave to a local organization to restore. Rice said he donated the logbook to an explorers' museum in Brighton. But the book seems to have disappeared. According to the National Maritime Museum in England, there is no explorers' museum in Brighton today.

Eventually, Rice ran out of money and energy for the restoration project. The donations and assistance he had hoped for did not materialize, and SCRAP faded into inactivity.

So Rice sadly decided, in 1988, that he would do better to pass *Sea Dart* along to someone who could complete the repairs and restoration he had started. He placed an advertisement in a regional sailing publication:

Sea Dart

Yes, Tristan Jones' boat, made famous in *Incredible Journey* [sic], is available to the right person. Needs a major refit. Now on San Juan Island. Conditions apply to gift. Call for info. Mark 281-0983.

The conditions that applied to the gift were the same ones that Tristan Jones had outlined in his letter to Rice: the boat was not to be sold for profit, and it was to be used for the benefit of children.

"I was just the caretaker of the boat," he says. "It belongs to the kids, to society."

Part of the reason behind these conditions, according to Jones, was *Sea Dart*'s unusual status with U.S. Customs. She had never actually been *imported* into the United States, any more than she had been *imported* into Peru!

"None of the Customs paperwork was ever dealt with," Rice said. "That's why it couldn't be sold."

Sea Dart had been allowed to enter, somewhat as a person might be permitted to visit with a temporary visa, but not to immigrate.

One of the people responding to Rice's ad was Tacoma nutrition-center owner Ron Groff. Groff had seen *Sea Dart*, and Tristan Jones, toward the end of the book tour. He still proudly owns the copy of *The Incredible Voyage* that Jones signed for him in that appearance.

Groff asked diver and boatbuilder Steve Dyer to check over the boat, and when Dyer said it was likely to be restorable, Groff decided to purchase *Sea Dart*.

Rice agreed to sell her to Groff, who did have money to put toward restoration, but he wouldn't turn her over immediately. Concerned about the refit, and wanting to be sure of the purchaser's intentions, Rice specified that Groff must repair and restore the boat to a seaworthy condition within two years in order to take ownership.

Groff was sure that, working with Dyer, he could complete the job.

"It was the saddest day of my life when I sold her to him," Rice recalls. But he felt at the time that the sale was best for the boat.

Groff, who had sailed for thirty years and owned more than two dozen boats in that time, spent some $8,000 on materials and labor for *Sea Dart* over the next two and a half years. *Sea Dart* stayed afloat, but years of rough treatment and salt-air weathering had taken their toll.

The surface of the plywood hull was so roughened and irregular, Groff said, that it could not be painted again. Dyer recommended fiberglass to create a smooth exterior surface. Because the interior was also "pitted and messed up down below," they chose to face, or line, the boat with mahogany which Dyer ripped into narrow strips and fitted into the inner curves of the cabin. Rice's patient sanding and painting were covered over.

Groff replaced the destroyed mast with one from a catamaran, and acquired some used sails: a jib and a brightly striped mainsail. He retrieved the bilge keels from Orcas Island.

They built a new doghouse to replace the one sawed off in New York. Unfortunately, Groff says, the new structure was built with interior mahogany plywood, perhaps to save money, since the area was to be glassed over. But the doghouse was not fiberglassed, as events turned out, so it suffered severe water damage in a short time. Plies separated and peeled into shabbiness.

Ron Groff with the bare, scraped hull of *Sea Dart* as he started his refit. PHOTO FROM RON GROFF COLLECTION AT IDAHO DEPARTMENT OF PARKS AND RECREATION.

Sea Dart at Gig Harbor, glassed and painted, her keels retrieved from Orcas Island and a new mast in place. PHOTO FROM RON GROFF COLLECTION AT IDAHO DEPARTMENT OF PARKS AND RECREATION.

Tristan Jones, having gone on during the 1980s to other adventures on *Outward Leg* and *Henry Wagner*, had settled in Thailand by this time. He and Groff corresponded over the next few years about plans for *Sea Dart.* Jones wrote in July, 1989:

"I was delighted to get, through Sailor's Bookshelf, the pictures of *Sea Dart.* It is a pleasurable relief to know that she's in good hands and once again in fettle. For years I've been trying to trace her, but to no avail until your news arrived. Who owns her now? I hope she's wearing the British Red Ensign; legally she must, as she's in the U.S.A. under a special non-importing dispensation from U.S. Customs at New York. So far as I know she's still registered as British in *Lloyd's Register of Yachts.*"

These comments are interesting in that Jones said he had lost track of *Sea Dart* after his extensive dealings with Rice and Feigelson. Nine years had passed, however, since he turned over the boat to them; so if they had not kept in contact, he may have assumed she had been passed along again. And, of course, *Sea Dart* had never been listed in *Lloyd's Register of Yachts.*

Groff arranged for Jones to give a slide presentation in Tacoma in mid-October, 1990, which Jones described as "highlights, places and people from a quarter of a century of sea-roving, everywhere, on seven seas and six continents."

In between writing that letter and traveling to Tacoma, Jones flew to Romania to become "Commodore of the Constanta [sic] Marina, which controls all yacht traffic in and out of the River Danube."

Groff's intention in 1989-90 was to donate *Sea Dart* to a chapter of Sea Scouts, and his early arrangements for Jones' lecture proposed a handing-over ceremony that might be filmed for a sailing video-magazine. But Jones' schedule, as he pointed out in a June 27 fax, was tightening because of his commitment in Romania.

"I will now be able to be at Tacoma on October 10th, to fly on to Thailand for a month or so about the 14th of October. Sunday is a 13th. We shouldn't hold any ceremony then for *Sea Dart.* I don't mind, but she's a bit superstitious, as are most well bred ladies, of course. Best on Saturday 12th.

"Can we do this? I hope so as any other time is impossible. I shall take the chance to discuss with you my plans for a tour with *Sea Dart* next year on behalf of Atlantis Society and the Sea Scouts."

But when Groff offered *Sea Dart* to the local scouts, they turned down the gift, because, he says, they didn't want to deal with maintenance of her wooden hull.

Groff and Jones worked out an agreement under which Groff could use the boat personally and care for it. He would make *Sea Dart* available when Jones needed to take her on tours or other promotional work. Groff was keeping *Sea Dart* at a marina in Olympia at that time. He continued to work on her, and his family used the boat now and then.

Jones' Atlantis Society tour never materialized.

In October, some 300 people in Tacoma came to hear Jones' stories and see his slides of voyages in various parts of the world. The appearance was videotaped in part, but the tape went to black in the middle of the presentation when the slide projector malfunctioned. The part that remains, however, shows that while Jones claimed not to be a photographer, his subject matter was often such that a bad photograph was next to impossible. The slides of his boats at sea, and the few he showed of *Sea Dart*'s journey to Lake Titicaca, were dramatic. Unfortunately, some of them also showed the damaging effect of time and poor storage conditions.

The adventure with *Sea Dart* across South America was only a brief chapter in Jones' lecture presentations by this time. He was much more voluble about his trips in *Outward Leg* and his current ventures in Thailand.

That winter, late 1990 to early 1991, Jones spent in Romania.

Reese Palley, who invited him to Romania, recalled in *Cruising World* magazine after Jones' death:

"I innocently sought to convert an ancient little harbor built by Constantine on the Black Sea into a modern Romanian marina. The project was beset by pettiness and obstacles. In trying to deal with this I came to believe that only a Tristan Jones could smash through the barriers daily set upon us. I asked him to come to Romania and be the commodore of the Constanza Yacht Club and the captain of the port. His job, which he accepted with a joyous glint in his eye, was to get these recalcitrant folk into shape.

"He stormed into Romania on his one good leg and set about, as only he could, making a silk purse out of a sow's ear. He spent the worst winter of his life in that small harbor roaring up and down the docks in his wheelchair, spreading panic and terror. In the spring he confessed to me that, despite towering rages and brutal tantrums, the battle was lost. Because I had seen him through worse times, I was curious to know how he had failed to conquer mere bureaucrats when he had so often and so handily conquered the gods themselves.

"'I'll tell you, boyo, the gods were easy. They stood and fought. With the Romanians it was like jousting with shadows. The worst enemy I never bested.'

"But years later his memory was still burned with the branding iron of fear into the sailors of Constanza. When I would go down to the harbor to look after my vessel, awkwardly stilted on the hard, their mouths would whisper half in terror, half in awe, 'Where is Captain Jones?' But their eyes really would be saying, 'God grant that he never returns.'"

Groff and Jones continued their correspondence, and Jones' Atlantis Society newsletter continued to outline his health problems and sailing projects. Groff sent him information about vitamin E and its anti-clotting properties, and Jones returned the page with a heartrending note: "Leg amputated above knee. Bloody oh bloody! Please send, Groff. God Bless!"

Sea Dart was still near Olympia, and Groff and his family continued to visit her over the next few years. In March 1995, Groff decided to move her closer to home, to Gig Harbor. After mooring her for a year at Stanich Dock, he anchored her offshore. He said he had a cover made for her, but even under cover the replacement doghouse suffered damage. And *Sea Dart* took on water. Reports that she had sunk in harbor, however, appear to have been exaggerated.

"She didn't sink," Groff said, feeling as Mark Rice did that he got some bad press along the way. "Water seeped in where it leaked around the rudder post." He said he set an automatic bilge pump to work, and that he regularly pumped the boat out. At most, according to Groff, there may have been twenty to thirty gallons of water in *Sea Dart*'s shallow bilge.

"I would never let water touch the mahogany work," he declared.

But by 1996, Groff had decided he must part with *Sea Dart*. He reasoned that since he literally "couldn't give it away," he would offer the boat for sale. While her intrinsic value might be low, he knew she might be worth as much as $20,000 to a collector. He felt he needed to recover what he saw as his investment in her — $10,000 or more in repairs, moorage fees and other expenses.

Once again *Sea Dart* waited, this time on the waters of Gig Harbor, to begin the next stage in her voyage through the Pacific Northwest.

XI. Rescued and Restored

Rick Segal says he had just purchased the latest Tristan Jones book at the 1996 Seattle Boat Show when another fan asked him where to find Jones' books. Segal directed him to the appropriate area in a bookseller's booth.

Then Segal heard the other man casually mention that he knew where *Sea Dart* was.

Segal stopped the man.

"You know where *Sea Dart* is?"

"She's at Gig Harbor Yacht Sales."

Segal headed immediately to the boat dealers' booth.

"You've got *Sea Dart*?" he asked their representative.

"Yeah, we've got it."

"I'll come see it tomorrow and buy it," Segal told him. "I'll walk on the boat and give you a check."

Of course, it wasn't quite that simple. But after a brief flurry of negotiation, Rick Segal bought *Sea Dart* from Ron Groff, through Gig Harbor Yacht Sales, for $12,500.

Groff included a clause in the agreement which allowed him the possibility of buying back as much as a half-interest in *Sea Dart*.

Segal, a programmer manager at Microsoft, in his mid-thirties at the time, had sailed for a few years, mostly on Puget Sound. Thrilled with his acquisition, he arranged to have *Sea Dart* pulled from Gig Harbor and brought to Seattle. Her first stop was Canal Boat Repair; later he had her moved to Northwest Yacht Repair on Lake Union.

In the beginning, Segal intended to restore *Sea Dart* for himself, and sail her for the pleasure of owning the historic boat. Like Rice and Groff, Segal had read all of Tristan Jones' sailing books, and had enjoyed an escape from computer programming through the Welshman's tales.

"I would have enjoyed owning and sailing her and saying, 'Yes, I have Tristan Jones' boat,'" he said later.

Segal recognized that Tristan Jones' stories had to be taken with a grain of salt, but the awe he felt for the sailor's verifiable feats was apparent.

"Assume that fifty per cent [of Tristan Jones' tales] is pure BS," he said. "Take all that out, and sit in the boat and think.

"Visualize the boat in the Panama Canal, and you're hustling to find help getting through. Or hauling it up the Andes.

"It puts 'I can't find a caffé latte' in perspective."

By 1998, Segal had retired from Microsoft to do some consulting and to work on the 32-foot sailboat he kept moored in Elliott Bay.

Segal agreed to Groff's terms, which included the possibility of Groff's retaining an interest in the boat if it were *sold* again — but if it were donated, Groff would not benefit financially.

When Segal viewed a videotape of Tristan Jones' instructions to Groff, he concluded that *Sea Dart*'s sale had taken place against Jones' wishes. Although Groff had 'rescued' the craft and restored her part-way, the proviso that she should go to a children's organization had not been carried out. He had not realized a profit from the sale, only recovered his expenses; but Groff's contention that he "couldn't give her away" notwithstanding, Segal felt strongly that Jones' wishes had been disregarded.

He had already begun the refit that would set *Sea Dart* properly afloat.

Northwest Yacht Repair, where he had his own boat worked on, normally caters to yachts of forty feet and larger. *Sea Dart* was not much bigger than some of their tenders. But they treated her with the care due a celebrated lady, and moored her in a corner close to the office. First-class marine carpenters performed what owner Greg Allen calls fairly extensive rot repair, replacing about a third of her hull below the waterline and just over three feet of the keelson, the heavy lengthwise timber that runs above the center keel.

They also replaced the plywood on her bottom, using a new high-quality marine plywood with many laminated layers; they rebuilt the motor well, and painted the bottom.

Carpenter Sam Stern was amused to note big wormholes in *Sea Dart*'s bottom, a result of her several years in tropical waters. He found it funny because Jones was adamant that *Sea Dart*'s hull was so thoroughly protected with paint and other coatings as to be utterly wormproof. The worms, burrowing into the wood during her time in South America, would not have survived in the colder northern waters where she was moored afterward, but they had left their mark.

Meanwhile, having learned that *Sea Dart* was supposed to have been used for the benefit of children, Segal began searching for an organization to take her. Like Rice and Groff before him, he was dismayed to find out how hard it could be to find an organization that wanted to keep and care for the little wooden boat.

He offered her to the Center for Wooden Boats; but, he said, they wanted to place her in a museum setting. Jones had been particularly clear on that point. He had specified that a museum was no place for *Sea Dart*. Other wooden-boat organizations also turned down the donation, as did the Sea Scouts again.

But Segal was determined to put the boat where she should be, to "get some closure" to the situation and fulfill Tristan Jones' wishes. "To correct something for a guy who's dead and can't do it himself," as Segal expressed it.

He had previously posted notes on the Internet asking for information about *Sea Dart*'s history, and by early 1997 he was in e-mail communication with *Sea Dart*'s former owner, Ron Reil. Reil by that time was teaching in Boise, Idaho.

Learning that Segal owned *Sea Dart*, Reil offered him a bell, engraved with "*Sea Dart* 1965," that had once been on the boat. Segal countered by offering him the boat to go with the bell. Reil declined, since he felt his adventures at sea were done and he couldn't properly maintain *Sea Dart*.

Through their e-mail conversations, Segal and Reil agreed to work out what was best for *Sea Dart*. They discussed the disposition of the boat in a phone conversation, and Reil next got an article published in *The Idaho Statesman* (Boise) which included a request that organizations which worked with children submit their proposals to him. Reil recalls he had "four good proposals from various church groups, plus the state proposal." Once he had them all in written form that summer, he drove to Seattle with his teenage daughter and one of her friends to meet with Segal and review the plans.

They chose a proposal from the Idaho State Department of Parks and Recreation, which would put *Sea Dart* on the water as part of a state boating safety education program.

"They were the clear winners, hands down," Reil said, "and would share the boat with all the organizations involved. It is supposed to be a cooperative effort to benefit all."

Idaho boating statistics make clear the fact that tens of thousands of people spend time on the lakes and rivers of the state; and Idaho has a port at Lewiston which receives ocean-going vessels that come up the Columbia River. But to many people, Idaho seems at first an unlikely choice of location for a craft such as *Sea Dart*.

Dan Schworer commented on the choice in the Seattle-published sailing magazine *Northwest Yachting*. Quoting the Parks and Recreation press release about the agency's plans for *Sea Dart*, he wrote:

"Now, isn't this nice. One of the most famous sailing boats of all times (a recreational boat at that) and it ends up in Idaho. Sure we think it's great for Idaho, and Idaho being part of the Northwest, we hold nothing against that fair state, where we've done some excellent boating of our own. But, for God's sake, it isn't even on the water! We're talking about an ocean going vessel here, not some ski boat. Wasn't there one of Lewis and Clark's old canoes lying around somewhere that could have worked just as well?

"Sour grapes aside, what really steams us about this whole thing is not that Idaho got the *Sea Dart*, but that Washington State let it slip through their hands. Think about all those other great vessels out there,

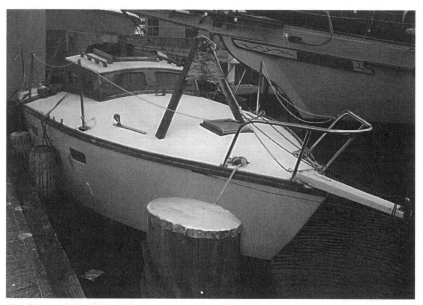

Sea Dart, sail-less in Seattle, on Lake Union. PHOTO BY RICK JUST.

Rick Segal (left) with Dave Okerlund and Ann VanBuren of the Idaho Parks and Recreation *Sea Dart* team. PHOTO BY RICK JUST.

Rick Just in the companion hatch on board *Sea Dart*. PHOTO BY ANN VANBUREN.

just rotting away in some Puget Sound boatyard or marina, which, with a little care and money, could be brought back to life to tell their stories to future generations.

"No, we turn our backs on such craft (and organizations like the Wooden Boat Foundation in Port Townsend and the Center for Wooden Boats in Seattle) . . . while vessels of true meaning and worth slip into extinction (or go to Idaho, which is pretty much the same thing) . . . ."

But Segal felt strongly that Idaho Parks and Recreation "cares a lot about what they're doing." He and Reil were sure that Idaho was the best place for *Sea Dart*.

By the time Idaho Parks and Recreation took possession of *Sea Dart*, Segal had spent thousands on the refit. There was still work to be done, but it was relatively minor. She was no longer taking on water, and she was beginning to look perky in her corner of the dock.

Segal estimated that he had put about $12,000 into repairs for *Sea Dart* in the short time he owned her. He 'sold' her to the State of Idaho for a dollar.

"It's the right thing to do," he said. "Not enough times in our short time on the planet do we get the chance to do that. It's pure."

He added that he was looking forward to attending her launch in Idaho, seeing her sail, and seeing *Sea Dart* at work helping the children who will benefit from her new career.

When Mark Rice learned about *Sea Dart*'s move to Idaho, he said, "I'm happy that it's going to be used properly. Tristan Jones would absolutely love that!"

And *Sea Dart* waited, bobbing ever so slightly on the cool waters of Lake Union, surrounded by grand yachts and two-story houseboats, protected from the elements by a plastic tarp. She was the sum of all her voyages, her unlikely presence a victory over the odds that face small boats and oceans and sailing dreams.

Tethered to that dock in Seattle, she was also the result of Mark Rice's finding her and his loving attempt to reclaim her from abandonment; Ron Groff's support for Tristan Jones and his further work on the boat; Rick Segal's insistence on owning and repairing her, and his willingness to give her up to fulfill a dead man's wishes. She had passed from one pair of caring hands to another.

Her mast was stored along a railing on the bank; her hull was smooth and white; and her new voyage was about to begin.

XII. Sailing Idaho

"It's like getting the *Spirit of St. Louis*!" Idaho Department of Parks and Recreation director Yvonne Ferrell said of acquiring *Sea Dart*. And not only getting the historic craft, but being mandated to *use* it, not set it in a museum.

Sea Dart's new home may take on a museum-like aspect, however, as stories and memorabilia from her past adventures surface to be collected and passed along to a new generation of sailors and other people fascinated by her story.

Rick Just, Idaho Parks and Recreation communications program manager, was put in charge of the boating safety education program. He collected *Sea Dart's* papers, provided information to the media about her new role and undertook the effort to make sure the boat and the program would be self supporting.

Soon after the announcement that *Sea Dart* would be coming to Idaho, he heard from a woman named Nicky Pleas. She had lunched with Tristan Jones when he and *Sea Dart* were making their way through the Panama Canal in 1973, some 16 years before she moved to Sandpoint, Idaho, on the shores of Lake Pend Oreille.

Later, Just received a unique donation to the project from an Anchorage, Alaska, man who had traveled to Thailand in 1997. Jim Foster had expected to find a Tristan Jones museum in Phuket; instead, he found Jones' house abandoned and open to the weather. In one corner was a pile of odds and ends that obviously had belonged to Jones. He left a note with his name and address, and took two items: one formerly white mesh brimmed hat (seen in some of the last photos of Jones), and a wooden leg with a Topsider deck shoe on the foot. He commented to Just that he ran into one problem on the flight home: the overhead stowage bins didn't have much leg room! He sent the leg and the hat to Just, and they will be displayed as part of *Sea Dart's* history.

In May 1998, when Northwest Yacht Repair needed to make room at their dock for a 111-foot yacht coming in, it was Just who went to Seattle to transport *Sea Dart* to her temporary quarters at Farragut State Park.

Just got *Sea Dart* out of her corner at Northwest Yacht Repair, where the big yacht waited to slide into place, and had her hauled across the lake to pull out at another marina. He went into the office there to settle the bill as *Sea Dart* was being loaded onto the trailer he had brought over. The man in the office, busy with his calculator, asked where Just was hauling her. When he said she was going to Idaho, the fellow thought that was quite a trip. Just replied that it wasn't much for this boat. She had crossed South America . . .

"That's the *Sea Dart*?" In a flash, the man was out of the office and in *Sea Dart's* cockpit, murmuring, "This is *Sea Dart*! I'm sitting in *Sea Dart*!" and running his hands over her sleek hull finish.

Idaho might seem at first to be an odd home for a seagoing vessel, as Dan Schworer and other sailors commented, but it's not so unlikely as one might suppose. Lake Pend Oreille, in Bonner County, is the largest natural lake in Idaho and one of the largest in the United States, a question-mark shape 43 miles long and about 20 miles at its widest, a total of approximately 94,600 acres of water — and more than a thousand feet deep in many places. Other documented vessels sail there every year, on waters that never completely freeze over. The U.S. Navy has an underwater research facility at Bayview, near the south end of the lake, used for testing model submarines.

Farragut State Park, at the southern tip of Lake Pend Oreille, was Farragut Naval Training Station during World War II. Named for the

War of 1812 naval hero Admiral David M. Farragut of "Damn the tor-pedoes — full speed ahead" fame, the training base was a hive of ac-tivity from 1942 to 1945, as some 300,000 sailors learned the ropes of Navy life and moved on to ships of the U.S. fleet.

A half-dozen campgrounds and two large day-use areas now host campers, family reunions and scout jamborees. A network of trails serves cross-country runners in the summer and skiers in the winter. Almost all the World War II construction is long since gone. The Navy-built brig, however, is still solid. And its maintenance shed was just the right size to provide dry, secure housing for *Sea Dart* when she came to Idaho.

So *Sea Dart* waited once again, sitting on her three bright-blue keels in the maintenance shed through a long, hot summer.

In mid-September a boating program officer, Doug Strong, joined Idaho Parks and Recreation to care for her and transport her around the state to attend boat shows and other events, as well as to develop boat-ing safety education programs for children in the state parks and in schools. Strong, an avid sailor for many years, had once owned a boat much like *Sea Dart*, set up for ocean sailing. He sailed in the summer and talked about sailing and the sea with friends in the winter.

"It gets in your blood," he said.

An Idahoan who attended the University of Idaho and taught recre-ation management for several years at Washington State University just across the state line, Strong had also worked in boating education in the state of Washington, in a range of programs that included training for marine law enforcement officers and teaching disabled people (mostly adults) to sail. On land, he had worked in a city recreational program for disabled people.

Recognizing that *Sea Dart*'s size and construction present an inher-ent challenge when it comes to using her as a classroom for many people at once, Strong said he would most likely build a curriculum around her as a symbol and an inspiration. With careful planning, small groups may be able to combine onshore activities with time on the water.

One of his most effective teaching aids, especially in situations where he can't take *Sea Dart* herself, is a scale model built by Michael

Lake, at the time an inmate at the Orofino, Idaho, correctional facility. Built with exquisite attention to detail, the three-foot-long model includes chains at the bowsprit, self-steering gear, reefing points on the sails, even a typewriter and logbook on the cabin table.

During the fall of 1998, Strong moved *Sea Dart* to Stan-Craft/The Boat Shop in Post Falls, Idaho, for the next stage in her repair and refit. She sat proudly in one corner as skilled boatwrights created a new bowsprit of solid mahogany to replace the well-worn sprit she was wearing. They crafted a new doghouse, new hatch covers and companionway washboards; replaced a section of rub rail; and gave all her wooden trim a gleaming clear finish. Strong planned to involve volunteers later on in maintenance tasks such as painting the boat's bottom.

Like many similar projects, this restoration raises questions about what, for the purpose of historic preservation, constitutes *Sea Dart*. Idaho Parks and Recreation has chosen to restore her to sailing trim and keep the essence of '*Sea Dart*-ness' alive, but without trying to restore her to a particular historic moment. In Idaho, she will be a working, sailing craft again, equipped as she needs to be to sail into the future, her past documented to show where she has been.

Strong's base of operations is now the Idaho Parks and Recreation's North Region office just outside Coeur d'Alene. *Sea Dart* will be berthed in Bayview at the south end of Lake Pend Oreille and also she will spend part of the summer at moorings on the north shore of Lake Coeur d'Alene, close to both headquarters and the highway. Lake Coeur d'Alene, another jewel-like mountain lake, is 23 miles long with about 110 miles of shoreline. On its shores are several small towns, camps, parks and other places where Strong can sail *Sea Dart* right up to the docks for various types of programs.

By November, Strong felt that *Sea Dart* would "show well" in her planned appearance at the January 1999 Seattle Boat Show. And he had learned, as he began working with her, how excited sailors and non-sailors become at the thought, "This is *Sea Dart*!"

"It's amazing," Strong commented, "how many people say they've read all of Tristan Jones' books — people you'd never expect." His own introduction to Jones' tales took place when he was teaching at Washington State University, where he read some of the author's sailing

Sea Dart in Stan-Craft/The Boat Shop, Post Falls, Idaho, with carpenter David Kaschmitter at work on her rubrails — clearly showing she's only 5'1" from rubrail to the bottom of her keels. PHOTO BY LAUREL WAGERS.

The scale model even has reefing points on the sails and the correct self-steering gear. PHOTO BY LAUREL WAGERS.

articles and came to admire the single-handed sailor, the loner, the enduring personality that Tristan Jones presented to his readers.

Sea Dart did "show well" in Seattle, attracting a steady flow of visitors even though she was placed in a pass-through annex rather than in the main display area, her mast packed alongside her trailer. A small, bright blue sail was rigged on the Kingdome wall and kiosks displayed photos, books, and a brief outline of her 'incredible voyage'. And a new brochure introduced Team *Sea Dart*, the non-profit organization established to support her in her new career.

From Tristan Jones' postings in the early 90s to Rick Segal's initial search for *Sea Dart*'s background to Ron Reil's Web site and the research for this book, much of the low-tech *Sea Dart*'s recent history has involved the new technology of the Internet. So it is only fitting that by the time *Sea Dart* appeared in public again, she had her very own presence on the Web — www.seadart.org — where her news and history are gathered together.

A few short months after her bow at the Kingdome, on one of the most blustering days of the spring, Doug Strong and Rick Just took *Sea Dart* out on the water to check her over in preparation for her official unveiling. On that Tuesday in early May, they encountered snow, rain, hard winds, and hail that collected half an inch deep on the deck. *Sea Dart* handled the weather with equanimity. The sailors found it somewhat less enjoyable.

On May 6, 1999, *Sea Dart* — now sporting the identifier ID 0001 A on her bow — officially began her career in the Idaho campaign for boating safety at the Governor's Conference on Recreation and Tourism. She charmed everyone, from the children in attendance to the governor who welcomed her, to the press. She sailed beautifully on that perfect, sunny afternoon. Even the Coast Guard Auxiliary men who towed her to her berth at the end of the afternoon's festivities were all smiles.

"A year and a half ago," Rick Just told the conference participants that evening, "I fell in love with a lady . . . " He told them the story of *Sea Dart* and introduced Dave Okerlund and others of the original Team *Sea Dart*. Governor Dirk Kempthorne, who had taken office in January, made clear his pride in having *Sea Dart* in Idaho. He led the crowd in a toast to *Sea Dart* and her team, wishing them fair winds and following seas.

Sea Dart's calendar was filling up already, with wooden-boat shows and other events throughout the sailing season.

The State of Idaho provides funds for the boating safety education officer and for the program he develops, and Idaho Parks and Recreation has bought the truck and custom trailer for taking *Sea Dart* to her various engagements. Through Team *Sea Dart*, donations and other forms of private sponsorship will pay for her maintenance and for any future expeditions.

The prospect of future expeditions seems to spread before *Sea Dart* like the glittering waters of a mountain lake. For, like Tristan Jones, some of *Sea Dart's* 'crew' muse about unusual voyages. Rick Just has a Tristan Jones-like gleam in his eye and an adventurer's enthusiasm as he contemplates sailing *Sea Dart* up the Columbia River from Astoria, Oregon, to Lewiston, Idaho's port and link to the ocean.

And then, he says with a smile, there's the possibility of a trip to the Dead Sea, world politics permitting. A little shipping, a chat with the Israeli authorities, and *Sea Dart* could very well sail on the world's lowest navigable body of water, claiming for herself alone the altitude sailing record — high *and* low — after all.

Doug Strong sails restored *Sea Dart* on Lake Coeur d'Alene, May 1999. PHOTO COURTESY OF IDAHO STATE DEPARTMENT OF PARKS AND RECREATION.

Sea Dart's "Ports of Call"

(P) = portage/hauling

1960   Built at Blanks Boatyard, Stanstead Abbots, Hertfordshire

1965   Owner lived in Romsey, Hampshire; *Sea Dart* registered at
        Southampton

1970   Isles of Scilly — jumping-off place for start of trip around the
        world

1971   Barbados Yacht Club, Bridgetown, Barbados
        Gibbs Bay, Barbados

1971-73 Barbados
        Grenadine Islands
        Tobago Cays
        Palm Island
        Salt Whistle Bay, Meyero
        Bequia (sold to Tristan Jones)
        Willemstad, Curaçao
        Santa Marta, Colombia
        Cartagena, Colombia
        Limon, Colombia
        Bahía Caledonia, Colombia
        Islas Muletas/San Blas Islands: Mulatupo, Playon Chico,
            Porvenir Island
        Portobelo, Panama
        Colón, Panama

Cristóbal, Panama
Panama Canal
Balboa, Panama
Taboga Island, Panama
Perlas Group: Pedro González
Gorgona prison island, Colombia
Salinas, Ecuador
Callao, Peru
(P) Lima, Peru
(P) Pisco, Peru
(P) Ica, Peru
(P) Arequipa, Peru
(P) Paso Cimbral, Peru
(P) Puno, Peru

1974   Lake Titicaca: Taquila Island, other islands in Peruvian waters
Lake Titicaca: Isla del Sol, Kochi (Koati), Pallaya, Chuyu,
    Lauasani, Quebraya, Auriqui, other islands in Bolivian waters
Tiquina, Bolivia
Guaqui, Bolivia
Puerto Perez, Bolivia
Huatajata, Bolivia
Cachilaya, Bolivia
(P) La Paz, Bolivia
(P) Cochabamba, Bolivia
(P) Paso Siberia, Bolivia
(P) Santa Cruz, Bolivia
(P) Puerto Suárez, Bolivia
(P) Ladário, Brazil
(P) to River Paraguay
Mato Grosso do Sul, Brazil
Forte Coimbra, Brazil
Bahía Negra, Paraguay
Concepción, Paraguay
Asunción, Paraguay
Paraná, Argentina
Santa Fe, Argentina
San Nicolás, Argentina
Buenos Aires, Argentina

1975   Olivos, Argentina
           Montevideo, Uruguay
           (P) shipped to England; stored at Newhaven

1977   (P) shipped to Bayonne, New Jersey
           (P) New York, New York (Waldorf-Astoria Hotel)
           (P) Pittsburgh, Pennsylvania
           (P) Washington, D.C.
           (P) Cleveland, Ohio
           (P) Minneapolis, Minnesota
           (P) St. Louis, Missouri
           (P) Kansas City, Missouri
           (P) Denver, Colorado
           (P) Texas, Arizona, California cities
           (P) Portland, Oregon
           (P) Seattle, Washington
           (P) Tacoma, Washington
           (P) placed in storage, Edmonds, Washington

1980   (P) Friday Harbor, Washington
           (P) Snug Harbor Resort, San Juan Island, Washington
           (P) Inland, San Juan Island

1988   (P) Olympia, Washington

1995   (P) Gig Harbor, Washington

1996   (P) Seattle, Washington

1998   (P) Farragut State Park, Idaho
           (P) Post Falls, Idaho

1999   (P) The Seattle Boat Show, Seattle, Washington,
              January 15-24
           (P) Coeur d'Alene and Bayview areas, Idaho

Tristan Jones' Major Writings

Autobiographical books in chronological order:
A Steady Trade: a Boyhood at Sea
Heart of Oak
Ice!
Saga of a Wayward Sailor
The Incredible Voyage
Adrift
The Improbable Voyage
Outward Leg
Somewheres East of Suez
To Venture Further

Collections of sailing stories, somewhat autobiographical:
Yarns
Seagulls in My Soup
Encounters of a Wayward Sailor

On sailing:
One Hand for Yourself, One for the Ship: the Essentials of Single-Handed Sailing (1982)

Novels:
Dutch Treat: a Novel of World War II
Aka

Jones also gave many lectures and interviews, and wrote articles and short stories for magazines around the world.

GLOSSARY

Aft Toward the stern, or rear, of the boat from any given point.

Antifouling paint Poisonous paint applied to prevent barnacles and other marine organisms from attaching themselves to the boat.

Ballast Extra weight, placed low to increase the stability of the boat.

Beam Breadth of the boat at the widest point.

Bilge The bottom part of the boat between the keel and the cabin sole or floorboards, where bilge water collects.

Blocks Apparatus with one or more rollers turning on pins between "cheek" plates. Lines go through the blocks, for example, to change direction or reduce the effort required to handle a sail.

Boom A spar (pole) attached to the foot (lower edge) of a sail to hold the edge horizontal.

Bow The forward part of the boat.

Bowsprit A strong pole fixed to the stem at the bow of the boat, to which a jib or other foresail is attached.

Chine The line where the boat's bottom meets the side at an angle.

Chop Disturbed water with short, steep waves.

Cleat A fitting with two "horns" around which a rope is made fast.

Close-hauled Sailing with the boat pointing as close to the wind as possible with the sails hauled in close to the centerline.

Cockpit The space where the crew can sit or stand to operate the tiller. *Sea Dart's* cockpit is self draining.

Companion The boat's main hatch and the entryway surrounding it.

Cutter A boat with one mast, rigged to carry a mainsail (the large sail with a boom) and more than one headsail (sails forward of the mast), dividing the sail area between the front and back of the boat; *Sea Dart* was built as a sloop and later rigged as a cutter.

Danforth anchor A lightweight anchor made with two flat flukes pointed back along the shank and a stock (bar) through the crown where the flukes begin; it has greater holding power than many other designs.

Deadwood Wooden (or reinforced plastic) pieces in the centerline.

Dinghy Small open boat, in this case one used as a tender (crew transport to and from shore) to a larger boat.

Doghouse A raised section at the aft end of the cabin; it provides extra standing headroom in the galley area.

Fisherman (or fisherman's) anchor The familiar anchor design with two flukes and a stock (bar) set at a right angle to them on the shank.

Forepeak A compartment in the farthest forward point of the boat.

Galley Food preparation area.

Genoa A large, lightweight headsail that overlaps the other sails; used to catch light winds.

Gimballed Refers to compass, stove or other object suspended so that it remains horizontal no matter how the boat moves (using concentric rings which move at right angles to each other).

Gunwale The upper edge of the boat's side.

Hard A firm part of the shore.

Hatch An opening in the deck to provide access to the living or stowage area of the boat.

Hog A lengthwise piece fitted over the keel, where the planks immediately on either side of the keel are attached.

Hull The body of the boat, not counting mast, rigging, rudder or anything above the deck.

Jetty A structure roughly perpendicular to the shore, where boats can moor.

Jib A triangular headsail (on a cutter, it is set the farthest foward, and may be tacked to the bowsprit).

Kedge A small anchor, and the process of using the anchor to move the boat by taking the kedge ahead in the dinghy, returning and hauling or winching the boat toward the kedge; for example, to move a boat that has run aground.

Keel The lengthwise structural wooden piece that acts as the spine of the boat; the *ballast keel* is bolted under it. *Bilge keels* are bolted partway between the ballast keel and the chines.

Keelson A lengthwise structural wooden piece that parallels the keel, set directly above it.

Knot The measurement of speed at sea: one nautical mile (1.15 statute miles) per hour.

Lazarette Stowage compartment at the stern of the boat.

Mast The vertical spar (pole) to which the sails are attached.

Port The left-hand side of the boat as you face toward the bow.

Reach A straight stretch of river (or, in this case, of a lake); a "broad reach" is a point of sail with the wind coming from the rear quarter (not straight back).

Reefing Reducing the area of the sail, especially when winds come up. *Reefing points* are short, lightweight lines attached to the sail which are knotted around the boom when the sail is reefed.

Rubrail A narrow molding fitted along the edge of the boat at deck level to protect the hull. British term is *rubbing strake*.

Shrouds Wire rope attached to plates in the hull to provide lateral support for the mast; in this case chains fitted so as to provide lateral support for the bowsprit.

Skeg On *Sea Dart*, a triangular piece which projects behind the ballast keel and to which the rudder is attached. A skeg protects the leading edge of the rudder and helps the rudder work more efficiently.

Sloop A sailboat with one mast, to which a mainsail and one headsail (usually a jib) are rigged. A *Bermudian sloop* is the British term equivalent to the U.S. *Marconi sloop* rigging, which means that the mainsail is tall and triangular.

Starboard The right-hand side of the boat as you face forward (toward the bow).

Stem The forwardmost structural timber of the boat, attached to the keel.

Step (the mast) Set the mast in place. *Sea Dart's* mast is stepped in a square fitting on the deck.

Stern The after, or back, part of the boat.

Tack To be "on a starboard tack" is to be sailing with the wind on the starboard side of the sail(s). A boat is "on a tack" if it is moving and not actually turning (jibing or tacking).

Tiller The long-handled lever projecting into the cockpit; it is attached to the rudder at the other end. Moving the tiller turns the rudder to steer the boat.

Transom The flat structure across the stern of the boat.

Trysail A small, heavyweight, triangular sail used "loose-footed" — attached to the main-mast but not to the boom — in stormy weather.

Washboards Removable boards set into grooves at the companion hatchway to keep water out of the cabin.

Waterline A line along the boat hull at the surface of the water; the design and actual waterlines may be different depending on how much weight the boat is carrying and the salinity of the water around her.

Windward The direction where the wind is blowing from; or, as a sailing direction, toward the wind. (Although triple-keeled boats are expected not to perform well sailing toward the wind, Ron Reil described *Sea Dart* as going "like a witch to windward.")

Yawl A two-masted boat, with a tall mainmast and a much shorter mizzenmast aft.

Thank you:

Rick Just, Ron Groff, Ron Reil, Mark and Sarah Rice, Rick Segal, Doug Strong; Greg Allen and his staff at Northwest Yacht Repair; Lothar Simon and Sheridan House; Bob Tanner, the Idaho Department of Parks and Recreation.

East Bonner County Library (especially the evening staff and interlibrary loan) and libraries from Vancouver, British Columbia, to London; Peter Bursey and many other helpful people in Cardiff, London, Bridgetown, Romsey, Kansas City, Seattle, Friday Harbor, Boise and New York; *Classic Boat, Cruising World, The Journal of the San Juan Islands, Northwest Yachting;* too many Web sources to list here; and whoever made e-mail free.

Readers Diane Newcomer, Ted Bowers, Charlie Herron, Donna Parrish, Margery Pratt; also Susan Hampton, Nancy Herron, Janet Mershon, Greg Pratt, Seth Thomas Schneider, Bruce Thompson, John Tucker, Lee and Stephanie Wagers, Morton Zainfeld.

Tristan Jones, R.I.P